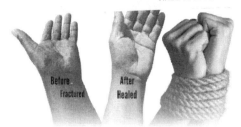

Before
Fractured

After
Healed

DON'T JUDGE ME BY MY
SCARS
OR
HOLD ME HOSTAGE TO MY
PAST

Dr. Orville R. Beckford Sr.

Published by:

ISBN: 978-1-958404-86-7 (paperback)

Printed in the United States of America.

First Edition.

WHERE YOU ARE COMING FROM IS HISTORY. WHERE YOU ARE HEADING IS DESTINY!

ENDORSEMENTS

Dr. Orville R. Beckford Sr. has crafted a deeply insightful and profoundly moving work in 'Don't Judge Me by My Scars, or Hold Me Hostage to My Past.' With wisdom drawn from personal experience and biblical teachings, Dr. Beckford invites readers to journey through stories of resilience and redemption. This book serves as a reminder that every scar, visible or invisible, carries a story deserving of understanding and empathy. It is a powerful call to suspend judgment and embrace compassion, embodying the timeless truth of 1 Thessalonians 5:21. A must-read for anyone seeking to heal and uplift themselves and others

Bishop Dr. Roderick Senior
Author and Pastor

This book is timely, challenging and thoughtful. Thank you Dr. Beckford for reminding us to be a more caring and non-judgmental community of love. May we all be inspired to use our scars and pain to encourage and bless others!

Bishop Dr. Leroy Greenaway Ph.D.

"**B**ishop Orville Beckford brings a wealth of experience and wisdom as a follower of Jesus and cutting edge leader. He has labored faithfully among God's people with a heart to serve. Readers of his new book will be encouraged and equipped to turn to Jesus for redemption, as they experience the scriptural narratives of restoration in a fresh way. Those who have been judged by their scars, or held hostage to their past, will find hope and healing as they digest the contents of this book. Be blessed on your journey through the pages of his work!"

Bishop Dr. Brian Sutton
North American Presbyter COGOP

One never quite knows where the story will lead when invited to be a guest on "Let's Talk with the Doc" hosted by Dr. Orville Beckford. One certain element of the media ministry is the precise confidence that the conversation will reveal the Faithfulness of God who is passionately centered in every story. Dr Beckford is a gifted and gracious voice who masterfully lays a safe foundation for each storyteller that leads to the resolved hope found in Christ. He is a delight to join with each invitation. I am excited to recommend his new publication (Don't Judge Me By My Scars, or Hold Me Hostage To My Past. This book will provide hope and healing for those who have been judged and prevented from moving past their past. This book will impact your life.)

Dr Catherine H. Payne Ph.D.
Global Missions Ministries COGOP

This book has created a vivid photographic image of understanding how to release the hurt, suffering and pain of the past. It lays out the decisive path to walk in and enjoy the pleasures of the future. The constructive model in this book is biblically based and practically explained. Read this book and your pain will become a pleasurable experience.

Bishop Ishmael P. Charles
Caribbean Field Director, Church of God World Missions

As a friend and spiritual colleague of Dr. Beckford, it is my pleasure to endorse the timely release of this great book, "Don't Judge Me By My Scars, or Hold Me Hostage To My Past." This book aims to break down the barriers we have set up against true fellowship with one another, as we hold others hostage to what they have done in their past and judge them by the scars they carry. I believe that God is pushing Dr. Beckford at this time because the Body of Christ is suffering from our inability to release our brothers and sisters from our judgmental scorn, so that they can go forward and do the work of ministry for the Kingdom of God. Thank you, Dr. Beckford, for your insight and spiritual acumen in releasing this important book at this time. We need it!

Prophetess Rev. Joycelyn Barnett

Everyone has either been judged by what they experienced in life, or knows someone who has been. Likewise, knows someone who has been held hostage to their past even after turning their lives around

Everyone has a past, and everyone who has made mistakes, made corrections, and moved on does not want to be constantly reminded about them or judged by them. If you have been judged by your scars or held hostage to your past, or knows someone who has been, this book is for you to read.

TABLE OF CONTENTS

FOREWORD

A native of the island of Bermuda, I enjoy reading books that are thought-provoking and relevant to everyday life. Serving in ministry together since 2022, I regard Dr. Beckford as a colleague and friend. I hold a Bachelor of Science Degree in Business Administration (Marketing), a dual Master's Degree in Management and Human Resource Development, and a Doctorate in Strategic Leadership. I am employed as the Chief Immigration Officer for the Government of Bermuda.

In my profession and as a Christian leader, I deal with people from all walks of life and understand the importance of getting to know people, their backgrounds, and circumstances before forming a negative opinion or erroneously judging them. Beyond observing people's actions, I have developed the art of intentional listening in order to empathize with others. On the other side of the spectrum, I have been judged without an opportunity to defend myself and know first-hand the crippling effect that this has on one's ability to progress in life without fear and intimidation.

I was introduced to Dr. Beckford through a mutual friend and served as a guest on his virtual program, *"Let's Talk with the Doc.*" Dr. Beckford's passion and creativity via social media are exceptional. He has a sound and strong acumen for interacting with people at their level, and his ability to draw out salient information to help individuals tell their stories is profound.

Dr. Beckford exudes excitement and has a genuine interest in people's needs, as evidenced by the kinds of guests he invites to his virtual program. He is a prolific preacher of the gospel and well-versed in the scriptures. He is a pastor and servant leader.

He is the author of a few books, the contents of which are proof-positive that he can articulate unique subjects that allow readers to obtain knowledge and apply learnings to real-life issues. He writes as a skilled teacher in a classroom setting who innovatively weaves repetition as a tool to ensure his core message is carefully understood.

In a brief conversation several months ago, Dr. Beckford mentioned that he was revising this book to include additional relevant information. He later asked if I would edit the updated manuscript. I did so. Having read the first edition, which is a little ebook, the additional information in this manuscript has enhanced the final product.

Whether we are consciously aware of it or not, the phenomenon of judging people by their outward appearance is undoubtedly quite common. Dr. Beckford aptly introduces the subject at hand and does not withhold the unfair treatment that can be meted out to people who are wrongfully judged.

The book is not external to its author. This means Dr. Beckford expressly speaks of his own life and exposes his personal scars, some physically visible and others emotionally invisible, and uses them to show the consequential judgments he has endured. Equally, readers will enjoy the several references to the bible, either direct texts or examples of people who were scarred or were prevented from moving past their past. My favorite part in the book is how Dr. Beckford hones in on key aspects of the lives of the bible characters and emphatically cautions his readers not to judge.

Beyond several cautions, Dr. Beckford identifies the primary reason for scars. Read the book to find this treasure. He also emphasizes the need for gratitude for where one was and where one is today or for the hope of a brighter future and better day.

I mentioned earlier, the author's skill with repetitious thoughts communicated in words. You could almost feel Dr. Beckford's concern and strong desire for better people and communities worldwide. The book is an easy and captivating read. It is applicable for individuals and groups, as a book study by book clubs or auxiliaries in the church, and for Christian and business leaders.

Without reservation, I wholeheartedly endorse this book. At the turning of the pages, readers' interests will peak. You will not be disappointed. Expect your thinking and behavior to be transformed. If you achieve this, you will be aligned with the author's aim to impact the world one book at a time. Enjoy the journey and happy reading!

Dr. Danett Ming Ph.D.

PREFACE

In a world that is quick to judge without knowing the facts of the real story, it is necessary to write a book. In the pages of this book, I delve into some of the complexities and injustices we experience as humans. This book, "Don't Judge Me by My Scars, or Hold Me, Hostage, to My Past," are stories many can relate to.

The Bible contains narratives written for our learning, reminding us that until one knows another person's story, one should not come to a judgmental conclusion. Everyone has scars. Some are etched on the skin and visible to the eyes, while others are invisible wounds that affect the heart and the emotion. As you navigate these pages, may you develop the compassion and ability to embrace those scarred by showing empathy rather than passing judgment.

By recognizing the lasting negative impact judging can have on another person, it behooves us to make 1 Thessalonians 5:21 a principle we follow. "Prove all things; hold fast that which is good." By doing so we will help others to heal and not contribute to their pain.

Thank the Lord for giving me the gift and ability to write and the passion to share on these topics. Thanks to my wife,

Deana, for encouraging me to keep writing. I appreciate her understanding of what it takes to write, and she allows me to continue doing so, though it costs her a lot more time alone. Thanks to Dr. Danette Ming for her contribution and editing. To everyone who encouraged and inspired me to write on the topic after I preached on the topic years before, may God bless you. And to everyone who reads this book, may God inspire and encourage your heart as you deal with your scars and checkered past.

Dr. Orville R. Beckford Sr.
2024

INTRODUCTION

Humans have a habit of judging others based on what they know about their past actions, behaviors, or mistakes they have made. They also judge others by perception or hearsay. Judging one by one's history could stifle one's growth, hinder one's success, or cause irreparable damage with lifetime consequences, whether one does it inadvertently or deliberately. When one is constantly reminded of failures, moral lapses, or the result and negative impact they have on their lives, it keeps them boxed in a bubble and hinders freedom to move forward. Not only does it prevent the individual from making progress, but it also inhibits building meaningful relationships. If one keeps playing the drumbeat of another's past, it can inhibit their ability to erase it from their mind, creating unnecessary hurdles for them to jump over.

Dealing with others who may have a history of making mistakes and or bear scars from their past, we tend to quickly judge what our eyes see without trying to gain knowledge of the cause of those scars and how they affect the lives of those who bear them. It is an unfair way to conclude something we are ignorant of. When one has a preconceived notion, one tends to use it as the basis of judgment, which, often, is wrong when proven. The Bible tells us to "Prove all things;

hold fast to that which is good" (1 Thessalonians 5:21). Some things must be proven, and others must be left alone without passing assertion or judgment. We don't know what we don't know, and therefore, we are admonished not to arbitrarily come to conclusions about what we do not know, and for things that we think we know, judgment should be avoided. Jesus addressed the after-effects of judging others.

> "Judge not that ye be not judged. For with what judgment ye judge, ye shall be judged; and with what measure ye mete, it shall be measured to you again. And why beholdest thou the mote that is in thy brother's eye, but considerest not the beam that is in thy own eye. Or how wilt thou say to thy brother, Let me pull out the mote out of thine eye; and behold, a beam is in thy own eye? Thou hypocrite, first cast out the beam out of thine own eye; and then shalt thou see clearly to cast out the mote out of thy brother's eye?" (Matthew 7:1-5).

Imagine if we made sure we were familiar with people's misfortunes before making a judgment. Consider putting yourself in the shoes of others, journeying with them for a while, getting a sense of what their world looks and feels like, and then determining, if that was our world, how we would want to be treated.

Would you want a second chance if you wasted the first one? If you have been healed from the pains of your past, would you want to be judged by those pains or to be constantly reminded of them? That's a calculation we must make and come to an honest conclusion as we reflect on judging others by their scars and holding them hostage to the history of their lives. How about understanding that some scars are for God's glory? We have seen throughout the Bible God allows his people to go through treacherous times and experiences while fulfilling his purpose in their lives.

People who bear scars under normal circumstances know where those scars came from and do not need to be informed or reminded. Those who make mistakes are aware of them as well. However, some believe the best way to keep you down is to keep pointing out your history to prevent you from excelling. Think about that in both Old and New Testaments. Few will meet the criteria if it requires people to be spotless and without blemishes to progress. The same is true of all the great men and women God has used throughout history.

As you read this book, something about your history might match what you read. Your past experiences in life might present hurdles you have been unable to climb over. Maybe people who know your story are unwilling to give you the green light to move on. However, it is too costly to allow others to dictate where you go based on where you have come from. Many matriarchs, patriarchs, prophets, apostles, and disciples we celebrate today all had stories of mistakes, struggles, and misfortunes. Some hit the proverbial rock bottom but rose to the top. Some have spent their lives evaluating others and miss the opportunity to assess themselves. The church has a history of causing scars, preventing healing from taking place, or at least slowing down the process. Some of you who read this book will identify with its contents. However, it will also give you hope and the impetus to rise above anyone or anything holding you hostage to your past or right now. Get ready for your sense of relief as you climb out of the dark places of your life, or be able to give a helping hand in pulling someone out of their dark places of memories and to move past their past.

CHAPTER ONE

TIME FOR ASSESSMENT

We are at a crucial point in the history of Christianity. If we are going to win the lost for Christ, we need to begin to see people through the eyes of Christ. What does it mean to see people through the eyes of Christ? It starts with the eyes of love, compassion, and care. Second, consider how you would want to be looked at and treated if you were in that same position. Third, seeing people through the eyes of Christ stimulates my humanity and triggers my desire to help. Jesus made it clear to Nicodemus that he did not come into the world to condemn it but to redeem it. Condemnation is easy because it does not require much of me. Jesus emptied himself of his glory so that he could sit with the average man, no matter his status in life. He rejected hypocrisy and falsity and despised those who placed themselves above others. Looking through the eyes of Christ inspires one to see how he can help to make a difference in the lives of others. Seeing our neighbor through Jesus' eyes will remove our blindspots so we do not exalt ourselves above another.

As I ponder this thought, what if I start to see people through the eyes of Christ?

The merciful, forgiving God, the one with great compassion for sinners, the giver of grace, and remover of one's past: What would be my attitude in my assessment, and how would I arrive at my conclusion? What could be worse than passing judgment without knowing the evidence of a case? Right now, as I write this section, it is on the news a gentleman has been exonerated after spending forty-eight years in prison for a crime he did not commit. He is said to be the longest-serving exoneree in the United States history. For forty-eight years, he lived under the label of a convicted murderer. Recently, a presiding judge set him free from the bondage of those who lied about him or judged him wrongfully. I wonder what their reaction is if they are still alive. Similarly, everyone should carefully assess their approach when judging others. Only Jesus has the right to judge because he alone is omniscient, and when he judges, his judgment is just.

Thinking of part (A) of this thought, "Don't Judge Me by My Scars," I feel a sense of pain for people whose scars have been judged without knowing the circumstances by which they have been scarred.

CHAPTER TWO

SCAR DEFINED

B y Definition (Merriam-Webster dictionary. A scar is:

1. A mark remaining (as on the skin) after injured tissue has healed.
2. A mark left where something was previously (Cicatrix), especially a mark left on a stem or branch where a leaf or fruit has separated.
3. A mark of indentation (as on furniture) from damage or wear; or a lasting moral or emotional injury.

Synonyms for scar include blemish, blotch, flaw, deformity, fault, imperfection, disfigurement, mark, and discoloration.

When considering the many ways and reasons one can be the victim of scars, one should be more careful before coming to conclusions about another person.

LOOKING BACK

As I thought of this, my mind returned to J. R. Martinez, the season 13 winner of Dancing with the Stars in 2011. Dancing with the Stars was a popular show that premiered on network television. Dancing with the "stars" was what it was.

I saw this man dancing, and as I looked at him, my wandering mind thought about what it must be like for his partner. During my quick, impulsive reaction to what my eyes saw, I felt terrible for them and imagined that if he was selected to dance on that show, there must be something uniquely special, gifted, or talented about him. My mind's eye could not see the gifts and talents he had and did not focus on the quality of his dance. His burned head, face, and arms stole my attention.

Out of curiosity, I searched to find out who this guy was and what had happened to him that caused those scars. I discovered that behind those (heart melting to the eyes) scars lie a soldier, a warrior, a man who fought for his country, a man who, despite those scars, was proud that those scars represent his patriotism and the sacrifice he made for the rest of us. Behind those scars lies a beautiful human being—a charming man whose character and personality were not reflected in what the natural eye could see.

Jose Rene Martinez was born June 14, 1983 (just about the age of my second son). In September 2002, he enlisted in the Army and underwent basic and advanced training. In 2003, J. R. Martinez was deployed to the Middle East and was in combat during the war in Iraq. Two months later, an unfortunate tragedy occurred. The accident happened when the left front tire of the Humvee he was driving ran over an Improvised Explosive Device. He suffered from smoke inhalation and was severely burned to over 34 percent of his body. This accident brought an abrupt end to his military career. However, the scars he bears will last for a lifetime. Some things in life you cannot erase even if you want to.

"JR Martinez spent more than two years at Brooke Army Medical Center in San Antonio, undergoing skin grafts and treatments for burns that covered 40 percent of his body."[1]

Despite being an Army veteran and burn survivor, he is an actor, motivational speaker, and best-selling author. What an unfortunate situation that scarred him for the rest of his life. "While the physical injuries were difficult to heal, JR Martinez's mental wounds were much tougher to overcome. But he is fine now, and he has inspired many people to overcome difficult moments in their lives". Do not forget this: God will put people in your life who will see the person behind the scarred body and treat you that way.

---

[1]

https://www.army.mil/article/50855/from_hospital_to_hollyw ood_a_soldiers_story

27

MY SCARS

I have visible scars in the center of my forehead—these scars happened many decades ago at about the age of 7 on a bright Sunday afternoon after dinner. A couple of my cousins and I were experimenting with cooking our little pot after becoming fascinated with the cutting remains of the produce used for dinner. I was a little older than others, so I took the lead in managing the process without understanding the dangers. Ignorance and innocence played a significant role in the attempt to cook and the tragic outcome.

Unfortunately, we took a large Milo can, placed all our cuttings in it, put it on the fire to cook, and did the most dangerous thing by closing it with the original cover. Having done that, it trapped all the steam inside the can, and it was like a time bomb waiting to go off with no air release.

With my ignorance and innocence, I checked the cooking progress. Excited to see the progress, I stood over the can and released the cover. It was like an erupted volcano sending all the steam directly into my face, which was no more than 12 inches away. That was a hard, youthful lesson to learn and one of the most brutal ways. Vividly in my mind, I can remember the experience as it happened. My entire face burned, especially my forehead, which was directly in the force of the steam as it rocketed out of the can. I cannot remember the extent of the pain I felt, but I was rushed to the clinic far away from my community to get immediate attention. It was a Sunday evening, so my local

28

clinic, about two miles away, would not be operational. Because of that, I was taken to another clinic about eight to ten miles away.

On leaving the clinic, my face had bandages everywhere. All that was visible were the two dots of my eyes and the space for my mouth so I could see, speak, and eat. Thank God for his goodness. He spared my eyes and mouth. I can clearly remember as I reflect on that horrifying day. Over time, as I grew and understood more, I realized that the scars were pronounced on my forehead and have gotten more visible with age. Those scars will remain there until I have a new body. We all have scars, some physically visible and some emotionally invisible.

CHAPTER THREE

THERE ARE MANY UNTOLD STORIES

I am sure there are millions of stories like that where people experience misfortune and are scarred for the rest of their lives by no fault of their own. Or because of ignorance or stupidity, naivete, and or innocence. People tend to focus on the scars they see and come to a conclusion without information on how they happened.

Every scar has a story; if known, it could generate sympathy and care instead of judgment. One may focus on another's imperfections because of the narrowness of the mind, the inability to feel compassion, or simply being cruel. The absence of the golden rule of "Do unto others as you would have them do to you" appears to be the farthest thing from most of our minds. Our physique naturally appeals to our sense of sight. And so, we can easily make wrong assumptions and conclusions about people.

The Lord told Samuel not to look at Saul's stature, height, or countenance because he had refused him. The

Lord sees not as man sees; a man looks at the outward appearance, but God looks at the heart (1 Samuel 16:7). Whenever we judge people by their scars, we lay the foundation of victimization that will lead to holding them hostage to their past. Why? because scars have a past and a history. Let us look at part B.

"DON'T HOLD ME HOSTAGE TO MY PAST"

We are inclined to hold people hostage to their past, even when God has forgiven them. I believe in the power of redemption, the efficacy of the cleansing power of the blood of Christ, and God's abounding grace. I believe the word of God as recorded by the Apostle Paul in Romans 5:20, "Moreover the law entered, that the offence might abound. But where sin abounded, grace did much more abound." That means wherever sin establishes borders, grace expands beyond those borders to provide abounding grace for the vilest offenders.

The Bible records many accounts of people held hostage to their past. Here is a glimpse into my past. I gave my heart to the Lord at the tender age of 10. I had infrequent asthma attacks; however, my church minister prayed for my healing and anointed me with olive oil, and the Lord healed me. For three and a half years, I had not had an attack. However, as my teenage years began to get a hold of me and I started to indulge with my other cousins and friends, I began to lapse in attending services and whatever I understood as a prayer life and a good relationship with Christ. Before I knew it, I had drifted far from the Lord and begun doing the things I knew I should not have done. I experimented on things I knew were wrong in living up to a Christian principle. Gradually, I kept drifting until I was utterly on the outside. Going to the movies then was abominable for a Christian, but I could not resist the temptation. Here is an interesting discovery I never thought of until this moment that I am writing. The first notable thing I did was to experiment with smoking cigarettes, and the last thing I did on my return to the Lord. The last thing I did was smoke the piece of cigarette I had in my breast pocket. Although it was fifty-one years ago, it is as fresh in my memory as five years ago.

Here is what happened. I went to the movie and bought two cigarettes on my way home. I smoked one but was consciously afraid to take the other one in the house with me, fearing my sister or mom would find it in my pocket if they were doing laundry. Searching every pocket before putting the clothes into the wash was the custom. If that happened, my mother would have many questions for me to answer. Then, I decided to get rid of it by smoking it. I was unfamiliar with smoking and, worse, inhaling. I saw regular smokers inhaling and felt it was cool, so I went all in on it as I tried to get rid of the cigarette. I had no clue how it could impact me physically. By the time I got in the house, I started feeling nauseous. It was so bad it took a long time to fall asleep. That was one of the worst nights I have ever had. However, that taught me a lesson I never forgot. Despite that experience, I continued to do the things I knew I should not be doing. I am reminded of the apostle Paul in Romans 7:11:

"For sin, taking occasion by the commandment, deceived me, and by it slew me." In verses 16-17, he continued, "If I then I do that which I would not, I consent unto the law that it is good. Now then it is no more I that do it, but sin that dwelleth in me." The next three years were the most checkered of my life. I was a young man on the loose.

I have done most of the things crazy teenagers did and some. I have never committed crimes or been arrested, so keep your imagination out of that direction. However, because of smoking and my other involvements, surprisingly, the asthma attacks returned worse than before. In retrospect, I conclude that God had healed me for his glory, but I was giving glory to the devil and not to him. Someone can learn a lesson from my experience. If you have been healed from a sickness or relieved from a situation and it returned, it's time to assess your standing in your relationship with God. God might be waiting for you to turn to him with all your heart and make yourself available for his glory. It is impossible to put the pieces of your life together before being able to identify them. I have said this to many people I have spoken to, "one of these days, God will reveal to you the mystery of your history." I believe God had called and healed me to become a preacher, and the devil knew it, though he is not omniscient. He is always looking for ways to derail the plan and purpose of God. Like it was in the beginning, so it is today. The devil goes about seeking whom he may devour and is relentless in his effort to hinder God's purpose from being fulfilled in your life.

The asthma came back with a vengeance. For the skeptics who will say if God heals you, the illness cannot return, you need to think again and let the Bible speak for itself. The familiar story of the man at the pool of Bethesda is one example to look at. Read the story in John 5. Jesus healed the man and told him, "Take up your bed and walk." However, we see in John 5:14 that Jesus met him in the temple and had a word of warning for him. "Afterward Jesus findeth him in the temple, and said unto him, Behold, thou art made whole: sin no more, lest a worse thing come unto thee." Those who believe that God wants to heal or make you whole to become a better agent of the devil make a big mistake.

Here is my testimony and experience. I told you about cigarette smoking at the beginning of my fall. I am not suggesting that it was the basis of my falling from grace, but it was another layer and a contributing factor in the process. It was also the last thing I did before walking to the house of God in total surrender. I am sure someone reading this will consider it ridiculous because he cannot associate smoking with unrighteousness or the means of backsliding. Some men find a way to justify the wrong, while others do all they can to avoid doing wrong. I am not giving a lesson of theological truth or relevance; I am sharing my experience and testimony. Listen to this: On July 16, 1972, at about 9:00 p.m., standing by a familiar place near a Duke Box, I spent many days and nights dancing when conviction hovered over me. I spoke to myself under the weight of conviction (I could see the church in the distance and heard the familiar voices of those I knew, singing the songs that previously brought joy to my heart). Whether audibly or deep in my spirit, I declared, "I am going to get saved tonight." That statement was synonymous with "I am going to turn my life over to the Lord tonight." The conviction was so deep I could not resist it. The intensity gripped my heart so firmly that I had to begin my walk to the house of the Lord.

God had it then that I was alone and didn't have to share my experience or decision with anyone. There was no one to ask why or whether I was sure. At this turning point in my young life, I had a piece of cigarette in my breast pocket. As I walked to the church, I lit and smoked that last piece of cigarette for unknown reasons. I did not consciously conclude not throwing it away. There was no superstition in my mind. Looking back, I wondered why I did not throw it away, but I concluded that God wanted me to close the chapter. Ironically, this is July 8, 2023, as I write this reflection. Since then, I have not smoked another cigarette or any other of its type for 51 years. Here is one of the most amazing experiences in this reconciliation process with the Lord. Remember I told you about the return of asthma when I walked away from the Lord? Sometimes, God uses things to get our attention and reminds us of what it means to be faithful to our words when we promise to serve him. He often heals us for his glory, not just that we can be better. It took a while for me to realize that.

Since I returned to my relationship with the Lord, I have not had an asthma attack until the day I put this in writing.

To God be the glory; he has given me a clean and clear lung to sing and preach his word without any hindrance or ailment. God had not held me hostage to my past. While one is not encouraged to do the wrong things, one should also be aware of the goodness and mercy of God and his willingness to forgive every repentant heart for whatever sins have been committed. God, in his wisdom and foreknowledge of the weakness and frailty of man, while living in the human, fallen nature of Adam, did not leave us without a way for restoration. There is the assurance recorded in the Epistle of John. "My little children, these things I write unto you, that ye sin not. And if any man sin, we have an advocate with the Father, Jesus Christ the righteous: and he is the propitiation for our sins: and not for ours only, but also for the sins of the whole world" (1 John 2:1-2). He cast my sins into the sea of forgetfulness and remembers them no more. That's one of the great things about God that's different from people in general. He moves you forward; he does not push you backward. He is not a hostage taker. I was well-known for my mischief and have used it to make many people's lives miserable, but don't hold me hostage to my past because God has set me free.

CHAPTER FOUR

SCARRED FOR GOD'S GLORY

LESSONS FROM THE LIFE OF JOB

One reason not to judge others by their scars is that many are for God's glory. Job's story began with God asking the devil about knowing him. God had confidence in Job, knowing he would be steadfast when facing adversities. We are told in Romans 15:4, "Whatsoever things were written aforetime were written for our learning, that we through patience and comfort of the scriptures might find hope." That verse is of utmost importance as we contemplate our experiences. The question becomes, what does God want me to learn from what Job went through? Can I use his situation as a guiding principle in how to deal with mine? In application of the verse as mentioned above, the answer is yes. Here is where the comfort of the Scripture comes in. Your pains, sufferings, scars, heartaches, grief, and brokenness are not exceptional. So, the lesson is to look back at what God has done and find comfort in what he can do. One can also find consolation in what the apostle Paul told the Corinthians in

1 Corinthians 10:13: "There hath no temptation taken you but such as is common to man: but God is faithful, who will not suffer you to be tempted above that ye are able; but will with the temptation also make a way to escape, that ye may be able to bear it." What if we know that the battles we fight, the scars we bear, and the storms we go through are because God has confidence in our ability to weather them all? I have had this conversation repeatedly with a friend who expressed trepidation to imagine that God could have that confidence in her and allow her to go through things like those because he trusted her not to quit under pressure.

There was something about Job that was notable by the devil. He saw him as a prime target because Satan concluded that if he could break the strength of Job by destroying his wealth, God would lose a reliable servant who had lost faith in God's ability to protect him. He was relentless in his effort to break through the protective barriers and failed in his attempts to hurt him. The Lord knew every move he made in his effort, hence the question. "Hast thou considered my servant Job, that there is none like him in the earth, a perfect and upright man, one that fears the Lord and departs from evil?" Job 1:8

The devil responded that Job did not serve God for naught but instead because God had edges around him protecting him from his attacks. Your adversary, the devil, wants you to feel that your foundation and fellowship with the Lord are strong only when things are going well. That was his concept when he deliberately told the Lord that had he not placed edges of security around Job, their relationship would have been shattered when he inflicted pain and suffering on him. The conversation continued, with God eventually removing some protection and giving the devil access to scar him. Finally, Job's world turned upside down when the devil attacked him from all angles. He suffered physical, mental, emotional, and psychological scars. He only had to hold on to his spiritual connection with the Lord and believe that material loss and the death of his family would not break him.

Although his human emotions caused him to wish he had not been born, he held his integrity and did not blame God for his suffering. Here is a summary of Job's approach, as recorded in the first chapter of Job. "Then Job arose, and rent his mantle, and shaved his head, and fell down upon the ground, and worshipped. And said, Naked came I out of my mother's womb, and naked shall I return thither: the LORD gave, and the LORD hath taken away; blessed be the name of the LORD. In all of this, Job sinned not, nor charged God foolishly" (Job 1:20-22). Many people have a false sense of security that if you are a Christian close to the Lord, you will not have bad experiences. Nothing could be further from the truth. History proves that. You can try to be careful and do everything according to protocol. However, if God sees something special in you that he can use to change other people's lives or use as an example to give others hope, he will allow you to make mistakes that you can learn from, then pick you up to show the power of his mighty hand.

I want everyone who reads this book to be aware that the devil will constantly come after you because you call on the name of the Lord. First, he will try to deprive you of the things God has blessed you with, and if he fails with those, he will come back at you physically. If he can't get you with emotional and psychological scars, he will try to hurt you physically because he desires to confuse you and weaken your faith. You become a target. If he targets your things and doesn't get you, he comes after your family and finally, he will come at you directly, or he might try it the other way around by coming at you first. He will change his strategy and method and use everything to get you down. Your family is not off-limit when he is determined to impact your life negatively. Look out for him; he will come in at whichever door he can gain access to.

Job had scars of all types during his attacks but kept his integrity in God. The devil underestimated what Job's reaction would be; however, as soon as he realized that his first attempt did not work, he returned to God and requested to touch him physically. He wanted to scar him because he said to God, "Skin for skin, yea, all that a man hath will he give for his life." Job 2:4, the second attempt, did that work. Looking from the outside, not knowing the conversation between God and the devil concerning Job, skeptics concluded that something had gone wrong with his relationship with God. Today, we face the same situation, judging what we do not know. In the process, something unique happened. Job's friends could not understand how this happened to him; they thought he must have done something wrong, so they confronted him. When Job's friends came to see him and knew of his relationship with the Lord, however, they could not understand under what condition he could be experiencing such suffering and loss, except he had violated God's laws and walked away from his statutes. The first thing that popped into their minds was to judge him by his scars. The narrowness of the human mind drives him to conclusions without facts. It is a good reason we are admonished in 1 Thessalonians 5:21: "Prove all things; hold fast to that which is good."

Job's friends did three things right. One, they came to see him in his time of grief and loss. Two, they empathized with him in the situation. Three, they spent seven days accompanying him. However, their attitude changed when things did not turn around as anticipated. After accusing Job repeatedly, they justified themselves by pointing out the reasons for his suffering without any knowledge except speculation. By this time, Job had enough of their hypotheses and judgment. In chapter 16, verse 2, he said to them, "I have heard many such things: miserable comforters are you all." The worst thing that can happen is that the people you depend on to be your help and support in times of need are making your situation worse. Their actions did not affect Job alone; they also got God's attention.

The people around you can create an atmosphere of guilt and cause you to question your integrity, even when you know you have done no wrong. Not only did they accuse him of wrongdoing, but they asked him to admit to his sins and ask God for forgiveness. The only thing Job could think of during this time of judgment was his questioning God's will. People can make you feel guilty about things you have not done. Here is a prime example. While Job was emotionally and psychologically devastated by his experiences and wished he had not been born, the record shows that he did not blame God wrongfully but continued to worship him. Amid everything, he looked beyond the immediacy of his crises to a brighter future. If you have not read the story, I encourage you to do so for more essential details. We are not told that God coerced Job before his intense attacks. No angel came and ministered to him, but God knew him, and he also knew God. His knowledge of God was not a head knowledge or something on the surface, but it was rooted deeply in his relationship and understanding of who God was. Hence, he was able to make this declaration: "For I know that my redeemer liveth, and that he shall stand at the latter day upon the earth: And though after my skin worms destroy this body, yet in my flesh shall I see God: whom I shall see for myself, and mine eyes shall behold, and not another" (Job 19:25-27).

In chapter 42:7, the Lord expressed his anger against Job's friends. Job repented, not for sins as his friends encouraged him, but for doubting and questioning God. As I said, their attitude got God's attention, and he was ready to pass judgment on those who dared to judge Job by the scars the Lord allowed him to suffer. "And it was so, that after the Lord had spoken these words unto Job, the Lord said to Eliphaz the Temanite, my wrath is kindled against thee, and against thy two friends: for ye have not spoken of me the thing that is right, as my servant Job hath." The Lord continued to express his anger and demanded that they offer sacrifices. He said to them, "Therefore take unto you now seven bullocks and seven rams, and go to my servant Job, and offer up for yourselves a burnt offering; and my servant Job shall pray for you: for him will I accept: lest I deal with you after your folly, in that ye have not spoken of me the thing which was right, like my servant Job" Job 42:8.

The same man they all accused of sinning against God, the Lord told them to go and sacrifice before him and ask him to pray for them, or he would deal with them according to their folly. That was as fierce a rebuke as one could get. I want you to take note of the Lord's scathing rebuke and demand.

"So Eliphaz the Temanite and Bildad the Shuhite and Zophar the Naamathite went and did what the Lord had told them, and the Lord accepted Job's prayer" v.9. This is like the stone the builder refused that became the chief of the corner. The Lord allows some scars and others he may use for his glory. For others, scars may be the misfortunes of life. Nevertheless, don't judge me by my scars or hold me, hostage, to my past. Finally, a long, heartbreaking story with many twists and turns ended.

And the Lord restored the fortunes of Job, when he had prayed for his friends. And the Lord gave Job twice as much as he had before. [11] Then came to him all his brothers and sisters and those who had known him before, and ate bread with him in his house. And they showed him sympathy and comforted him for all the evil that the Lord had brought upon him. And each of them gave him a piece of money and a ring of gold.

And the Lord blessed the latter days of Job more than his beginning. And he had 14,000 sheep, 6,000 camels, 1,000 yoke of oxen, and 1,000 female donkeys. [13] He had also seven sons and three daughters. [14] And he called the name of the first daughter Jemimah, and the name of the second Keziah, and the name of the third Keren-hapus. [15] And in all the land there were no women so beautiful as Job's daughters. And their father gave them an inheritance among their brothers. [16] And after this Job lived 140 years, and saw his sons, and his sons' sons, four generations. [17] And Job died, an old man, and full of days. **Job 42:10-17 (ESV)** *In the end, Job's desire to give God the benefit of the doubt worked out in his favor, as he stated profoundly in chapter 13:15, "Though he slay me, yet will I trust him: but I will maintain mine own ways before him." If your ways please the Lord, he will make even your enemies be at peace with you.*

Our stories and experiences may never be like those of Job. However, we have a perfect example to follow when we are tested and scarred. So, instead of lamenting and anguishing over what you have been through that leaves you with permanent scars, be grateful to the Lord that you are here as a witness and a testimony of God's goodness, grace, mercy, and love. You cannot erase your past; some scars are not removable, but they can show others what you have been through and help them understand that God can do the same for them. There is nothing more significant than a living testimony. Do not allow those looking from a distance to dictate how you see and think about yourself. If someone chooses to judge you by your scars and hold you hostage to your past, let him have it. External carnal eyes cannot discover the inner workings of God. Resist one's effort to bottle you up in one's container of carnal thinking. Redeemed people give credence to the redemptive power of Christ and understand that God's grace erases every past sin that has been repented of, and he remembers them no more. Stand firm on the word of God recorded in Ephesians 2:1-2, "And you hath he quickened, who were dead in trespasses and sins; wherein in time past ye walked according to the course of this world, according to the prince of the power of the air, the spirit that now worketh in the children of disobedience."

Live with that understanding and keep looking through your windshield moving forward, though others may want you to focus on your rearview mirror. That will only become a distraction and might fulfill one's desire to derail you and prevent you from reaching your true potential or fulfilling your God-given purpose.

CHAPTER FIVE

JOSEPH'S LIFE: PUTTING THE PIECES TOGETHER

The story of Joseph is repeatedly mentioned across Christian platforms in every denomination. It is a long story with many twists and turns, but it is one of the most fascinating stories in the Bible. It is like reading a fairy tale. Without understanding God's unique and incredible work, one could be left mystified by reading that story. The perplexities involved and how they unfolded leave one in awe or bewildered by the unfathomable work of God. This story is in the book for the benefit of those who feel like if God calls one, his life should not be marred with struggles, suffering, and pain. Joseph was the eldest son of Rachael but the eleventh son of Jacob. God has a way of structuring his plan and purpose that supersedes human comprehension. God has them in the making before things materialize or enter man's mind. For a man to put the pieces of his life together, he has to look back to find them.

On the other hand, God puts the pieces together moving forward and allows them to fall in place. The Lord told

Jeremiah, "Before I formed thee in the belly I knew thee, and before thou camest forth out of the womb I sanctified thee, and I ordained thee a prophet unto the nations" (Jeremiah 1:5 KJV). David gave his version of his understanding of God's knowledge in Psalm 139:15: "My substance was not hid from thee, when I was made in secret, and curiously wrought in the lowest parts of the earth." One can conclude that God divinely orchestrated the entire story of Jacob, Rachel, and Joseph to come to fruition at the appointed time. The whole story begins in Genesis 29. Rachel was Jacob's first love, but after working seven years for her, Laban cheated and gave him Leah. He had to work seven more years for Rachael. Because Jacob and Rachael loved each other, they both hated Leah. "And when the Lord saw that Leah was hated, he opened her womb: but Rachel was barren" (Genesis 29:30). In looking at the working of God, one can conclude that he had strategically structured the life of Jacob, leading to Joseph as the eleventh child.

One cannot fully understand God's plans looking forward. However, looking back at the progression and seeing how the pieces fall into place, he can say, now I know what God was doing.

Imagine how emotionally scarred Rachel was and how desperately she wanted to be the wife who fulfilled all of Jacob's dreams. Use your feelings and emotions blended with your imagination and position yourself where she was. Merrill F. Unger, in his Bible Dictionary, says: "Barrenness, in the East, was looked upon as a great reproach as well as a punishment from God (1 Sam. 1:6, 7; Isa. 47:9; 49:21; Luke 1:25, etc.) ... The approach attached to barrenness, especially among the Hebrews, was doubtless due to the constant expectation of the Messiah and the hope cherished by every woman that she might be the mother of the promised Seed. To avoid the disgrace of barrenness, women gave their handmaidens to their husbands, regarding the children born under such circumstances as their own" (Genesis 16:2).

God never sticks with the norm of man's expectations, neither is he obligated in doing so. It appears God deliberately looked for barren women to open their wombs for his glory or made them barren until his appointed time. Where have we seen that before? God has a history of doing the same thing. It happened to Sarah with Isaac as the promised child. You can find the story in Genesis 20-21. How about Hannah after being ridiculed by Peninah? "And her adversary also provoked her sore, for to make her fret, because the Lord had shut up her womb" (1 Samuel 1:6). Her husband Elkanah tried year after year to make her happy by giving her the best of his meat, but nothing could remove the ridicule of Peninah. However, after travailing and prevailing prayer at the altar, God responded to her cry.

"And she was in bitterness of soul, and prayed unto the Lord, and wept sore. And she vowed a vow, and said, O Lord of hosts, if thou wilt indeed look on the affliction of thine handmaid, and remember me, and not forget thine handmaid, but wilt give unto thine handmaid a manchild, then I will give him unto the Lord all the days of his life, and there shall no razor come on his head" (vs. 10-11). The Lord heard and answered her prayer after she had been ridiculed and pommeled by Peninah. The result was Samuel, who became a stalwart in carrying out God's divine plans. The same experience is mentioned in more women, like the mother of Samson, in Judges 13. These are four great patriarchs of the Old Testament and the unforgettable sons God blessed them with. All of them bore the scars of barrenness, but God gloriously turned their lives around to the surprise of their antagonists.

What are the odds that Rachel, Jacob's first choice for a wife, became the last to bring forth children in his old age except by the pre-determinate plan of God? How long can you hold out to be scarred emotionally for God's glory? Try to wrap your mind around the scenario. Rachel had the twelfth and thirteenth children for Jacob, the eleventh and twelfth of his sons. She had to watch her sister Leah bring forth seven children to Jacob, two each from Zilpah, Leah's servant, and two from Bilhah, Rachel's servant before God opened her womb. She lived with the stigma of beauty but was barren. Every time these women had another child, the wound went deeper.

Not only was she distraught, but it is reasonable to believe that it also profoundly impacted Jacob. He couldn't break the cycle of God's plan. Jacob ran out of words and methods to bring Rachel comfort. She reached her breaking point, battered, bruised, and broken as she watched her blossoming years gradually fade. We have seen Leah's weaponization of her fertility against her sister and how braggadocious Leah was every time she had another child. When she ceased having children, she sent her maid in to Jacob, and she conceived twice. At this point, Rachel felt her only chance was to have a child by proxy. Here is the account of Rachel's desperation.

Genesis 30:1-13

And when Rachel saw that she bare Jacob no children, Rachel envied her sister; and said unto Jacob, Give me children, or else I die. And Jacob's anger was kindled against Rachel: and he said, Am I in God's stead, who hath withheld from thee the fruit of the womb?

And she said, Behold my maid Bilhah, go in unto her; and she shall bear upon my knees, that I may also have children by her. And she gave him Bilhah her handmaid to wife: and Jacob went in unto her.

And Bilhah conceived, and bare Jacob a son.

And Rachel said, God hath judged me, and hath also heard my voice, and hath given me a son: therefore called she his name Dan.

And Bilhah Rachel's maid conceived again, and bare Jacob a second son.

53

And Rachel said, With great wrestlings have I wrestled with my sister, and I have prevailed: and she called his name Naphtali.

When Leah saw that she had left bearing, she took Zilpah her maid, and gave her Jacob to wife. And Zilpah Leah's maid bore Jacob a son.

And Leah said, A troop cometh: and she called his name Gad.

And Zilpah Leah's maid bare Jacob a second son.

And Leah said, Happy am I, for the daughters will call me blessed: and she called his name Asher.

After Rachel had exhausted all options and clutched onto her two children by proxy, God was ready to release fertility in her womb. At the end of it, the blessings of God came in like cool water to a thirsty soul. What Leah, Rachel, and Jacob thought would never be realized happened when the fullness of God's time fully came. What was classified as a curse turned out to be the greatest blessing. Of all Jacob's children, his eleventh son and the first for Rachel brought him more happiness than all those before him. It is easy to understand why Joseph was so special to Jacob. Outside of what is believed to be God's divine plan, one can imagine what it meant to Jacob after what he and Rachel had been through.

Whether they attributed the opening of her womb to God or not, it is evident that Jacob felt overjoyed about Rachael giving him a son. There are three things to take note of. One is the healing of Rachel's emotional scars. Two is the relief for Jacob, who did not need to worry about her barrenness, and finding ways to comfort her. Three is the joy of having this son in old age. In combining all these factors, the love for Joseph came from a deep place in Jacob's heart. The experience was so gratifying he felt that he had completed his time with Laban. "And it came to pass when Rachel had born Joseph, that Jacob said unto Laban, Send me away, that I may go unto mine own place, and to my country" (Genesis 30:25). That statement reminds me of Simeon's request to the Lord after blessing Jesus. "Now lettest thy servant depart in peace, According to thy word: For mine eyes have seen thy salvation, Which thou hast prepared before the face of all people: A light to lighten the Gentiles, And the glory of thy people Israel" (Luke 2:29-32 KJV). Simeon asked for leave to depart the earth. Jacob asked for leave after God blessed Rachel with Joseph.

JOSEPH'S PERSONAL STORY

Joseph is another prime example of being scarred for God's glory. When one considers his story from birth leading to his achievement in Egypt, it is hard to conclude otherwise that this was all in God's plan. After the excitement of Joseph's birth and the departure of Jacob with the rest of his family, nothing was mentioned of him until he was seventeen years old. During that period, he appears to have developed a notable character. "As the child of Rachel, and 'son of his old age" (37:3), and doubtless also for his excellence of character, he was beloved by his father above all his brethren. This, together with the fact that he reported to his father the evil conduct of the sons of Bilhah and Zilpah, caused his brethren to hate him" (Ungers' Bible Dictionary p.606). The hatred grew worse because his father showed preference for him by giving him the famous coat of many colors. "Now Israel loved Joseph more than all his children, because he was the son of his old age: and made him a coat of many colors. And when his brethren saw that their father loved him more than all his brethren, they hated him, and could not speak peaceably unto him" (Genesis 37:3-4). Talking about being scarred for God's glory, this is a prime example. It didn't get better for him when he told his two dreams.

And Joseph dreamed a dream, and he told it to his brethren: and they hated him yet the more. And he said unto them, Hear, I pray you, this dream which I have dreamed: For, behold, we were binding sheaves in the field, and, lo, my sheaf arose, and also stood upright; and, behold, your sheaves stood round about, and made obeisance to my sheaf. And his brethren said to him, Shalt thou indeed reign over us? Or shalt thou indeed have dominion over us? And they hated him yet the more for his dreams, and for his words. And he dreamed yet another dream, and told it his brethren, and said, Behold, I have dreamed a dream more; and, behold, the sun and the moon and the eleven stars made obeisance to me. And he told it to his father, and to his brethren: and his father rebuked him, and said unto him, What is this dream that thou hast dreamed? Shall I and thy mother and thy brethren indeed come to bow down ourselves to thee to the earth? And his brethren envied him; but his father observed the saying. (Genesis 37:5-11).

Joseph's brothers went to tend to his father's flock and did not return as expected because they had gone to another location. Strangely, Jacob would send Joseph, the younger brother, by himself to go and search for his older siblings who had not returned as was anticipated. They were expected to be in Shechem. But they were in Dothan. It is easy to conclude that there was a lack of discernment or naivete where Jacob is concerned, that he ran the risk of sending Joseph to find his brothers, knowing they hated him. At the same time, Joseph was old enough to know that his brothers were hostile against him but was too innocent in his thinking to foresee the danger. One wonders, if Jacob was that protective of Joseph, how could he have taken such a risk? The conclusion is that God's timing cannot be derailed.

In reading about the life of Joseph and others mentioned in this book, you may picture yourself as having done all you could for your life to go in another direction, but here you are. Maybe you are asking yourself what you have done wrong or what you could have done better or differently. It might not be until you can look back and see the divine purpose of God being worked out in your life. There are things you will not understand or have answers for. Neither will others be able to give clear reasons unless they have been directed by the Lord. However, what he will do is prevent you from crumbling during the process by sustaining you with grace until you see his salvation. It might be the thing you feared the most that happened to you. That was Job's experience. This is what he said in his words. "For the thing which I greatly feared is come upon me and that which I was afraid of is come unto me" (Job 3:25). Be patient under pressure. God will help you to understand when the time is right.

Joseph's brothers did not expect him and were not where Joseph expected them to be, yet they recognized him from afar even before he came near them and conspired to slay him. Their communication about killing him indicates their widespread hate, envy, and resistance. "And they said one to another, Behold, this dreamer cometh. Come now therefore, and let us slay him, and cast him into some pit, and we will say, Some evil beast hath devoured him: and we shall see what will become of his dreams" (Vs. 19-20). It tells how deeply they were affected by the dreams Joseph shared.

They failed to discern that Joseph's dreams did not come from his desire to lord over them but from a deep place in God's divine plan. What God plans, he will preserve. You cannot kill the purpose that the Lord has predestined. Someone reading this book may have been in a similar situation where others tried to destroy what God has deposited in you. Some people have done all they could to Blythe or destroy the dreams of others, only to see them do better. The only one not surprised by these moves was God, who sees from the beginning to the end. At the same time, he orchestrated a way to bring it to fruition. At the end of the story, we will see Joseph affirm that God was in the midst of the process, working his purpose out. His elder brother Reuben's unlikely but not surprising intervention advocated against the shedding of his blood.

Nevertheless, he agreed to throw him into a pit and return him home to his father's arms. When he returned, his brothers turned their hate into a money-making scheme, to his surprise and dismay. Maybe Reuben was motivated by the guilt of conscience and wanted to be reconciled with his father, Jacob because he had committed adultery with his concubine. He knew how much Jacob loved Joseph, and returning him safely to his father could be of high value in rebuilding their relationship, especially if he told the story about the other brothers' intentions. Sadly, that was not the case. However, it aligns with the apostle's infamous verse in Romans 8:28. "And we know that all things work together for good to them that love God, to them who are the called according to his purpose." Joseph's scars, hatred, rejection, envy, and humiliation were for God's glory. He was not sold once, but he was sold twice. Despite his journey, he was in the favor of God. I often say your journey is not your destiny, but you cannot get to your destiny without your journey. Likewise, you cannot get the result without going through the process, which can be messy, challenging, and painful. Everything Joseph had been through was for the glory of God. If his brothers had an insight into knowing they were helping to make his dreams a reality, chances are they might be less enthusiastic about making it happen. While trying to kill the dreamer and his dreams, they inadvertently enhanced them. The Lord told the church of Philadelphia in Revelation 3, "I have set before thee an open door, and no man can shut it." Walking through the door might not be easy, but it is open.

Joseph was like merchandise being sold in Egypt. But he had to move from place to place until he got where God intended for him to reach. The Ishmaelites sold him to Potiphar. God blessed him while he served his master, and his master developed great regard and respect for him. There was something uniquely different about him that got the attention of his master. "And his master saw that the Lord was with him, and that the Lord made all that he did to prosper in his hand. And Joseph found grace in his sight, and he served him: and he made him overseer over his house, and all that he had he put into his hand" (Genesis 39:3-4). You can read the rest of the story in the chapter, and you will see that Potiphar's wife developed a crush on him and did all she could to get him in bed with her. As dramatic as the story was and as evil as one considers Potiphar's wife, it was how God would allow evidence in her hand that raged her husband to believe her lies. Joseph's reputation and character were tarnished by an evil woman who did not have her sexual urges gratified. She was embarrassed and terrified that a servant in her house dared to reject her advances. Out of his master's rage, he was imprisoned and scarred for God's glory.

> *But the Lord was with Joseph, and shewed him mercy, and gave him favor in the sight of the keeper of the prison. And the keeper of the prison committed to Joseph's hand all the prisoners that were in the prison; and whatsoever they did there, he was the doer of it. The keeper of the prison looked not to any thing that was under his hand; because the Lord was with him, and that which he did, the Lord made it to prosper. (Genesis 39:21-23)*

It is hard to imagine the mental, emotional, and social pressure he was in away from his brothers and the love of his father. Then again, God has a way of helping his people cope during the difficult times of their lives. He didn't promise that there would not be dark nights and treacherous days, but he promised never to leave you to navigate them by yourself. "When thou passest through the waters, I will be with thee; and through the rivers, they shall not overflow thee. When though walkest through the fire, thou shalt not be burned, neither shall the flame kindle upon thee" (Isaiah 43:2). Although Joseph was put in prison, he was placed where the king's prisoners were bound because that's where the opportunity would come for him to make connections with King Pharaoh. God did not only give Joseph dreams, but he also gave him the ability to understand and interpret dreams as well. For unknown reasons, Pharaoh was wrathful against two of his chief servants and had them imprisoned.

The captain of the guards placed them in the ward where Joseph would serve them. Maybe they were placed on timeout punishment only so that Joseph could get closer to finding favor with Pharaoh. On his assigned duty to serve the king's chief butler and baker, he noticed their countenances were not pleasant but rather sad. Out of curiosity and concern about what was happening with them, he was told they both had disturbing dreams, but there were no interpreters. Even in prison, being labeled a sexual molester, he retained his connection with the God of Abraham, Isaac, and Jacob. What people think or say about you is irrelevant to what God knows about you.

Joseph concluded that interpretations belonged to God and felt God would give them to him. He interpreted the butler's dream to the tune that Pharaoh would restore him to his position in three days, and when it happened, he should remember him. The baker's dream, however, was not in the same favor. He was told that the king would hang him, and both dreams were fulfilled as Joseph told them they would. Unfortunately, the butler forgot Joseph after he was restored to his original position. However, the saying goes like this. God remembers when others forget. The butler went about his business, happy to be released from prison, and Joseph was nowhere on his mind. Two long years passed without a word from the butler, but God was still working on his purpose in Joseph's life. It was not until Pharaoh had dreams that perplexed him and troubled his spirit with no one to give him the interpretations that God reminded the butler of the

Hebrew young man who helped him understand his dream and that of the baker.

Desperate to know what his dreams meant, he hastily called for Joseph to be brought out of the dungeon. God was ready to take him past his past, from the pit to the palace. He told the king that God shall give him an answer of peace. The dreams were complicated and understandably troubled the spirit of Pharaoh. Nevertheless, what is beyond human comprehension is below average for the Lord. The king was astounded by what he heard from the servant of God. The interpretation was crucial for the survival of the land of Egypt. Not only did he give the meaning of the dreams, but in the wisdom of God, he also gave him what strategic approach he should take during times of plenty and how to ration and preserve for the time of the expected famine. Remember, Joseph told him that God would give him the interpretations. It is reasonable to believe that Joseph could be sent back to prison once the king was satisfied that he had understood his perplexed dreams. But the breakaway from the wounds, bruises, scars, trauma, abandonment, humiliation, and distress was about to happen. His past was about to become a distant memory.

Genesis 41:37-46:
[37] And the thing was good in the eyes of Pharaoh, and in the eyes of all his servants. [38] And Pharaoh said unto his servants, Can we find such a one as this is, a man in whom the Spirit of God is? [39] And Pharaoh said unto Joseph, Forasmuch as God hath shewed

thee all this, there is none so discreet and wise as thou art: ⁴⁰ Thou shalt be over my house, and according unto thy word shall all my people be ruled: only in the throne will I be greater than thou. ⁴¹ And Pharaoh said unto Joseph, See, I have set thee over all the land of Egypt. ⁴² And Pharaoh took off his ring from his hand, and put it upon Joseph's hand, and arrayed him in vestures of fine linen, and put a gold chain about his neck; ⁴³ And he made him to ride in the second chariot which he had; and they cried before him, Bow the knee: and he made him ruler over all the land of Egypt. ⁴⁴ And Pharaoh said unto Joseph, I am Pharaoh, and without thee shall no man lift up his hand or foot in all the land of Egypt. ⁴⁵ And Pharaoh called Joseph's name Zaphnathpaaneah; and he gave him to wife Asenath the daughter of Potipherah priest of On. And Joseph went out over all the land of Egypt. ⁴⁶ And Joseph was thirty years old when he stood before Pharaoh king of Egypt. And Joseph went out from the presence of Pharaoh, and went throughout all the land of Egypt.

Take a look at that last part of verse 46. "Joseph went out from the presence of Pharaoh and went throughout all the land of Egypt." Just a few days before, he was in a prison dungeon. Now, he is moving all through the land of Egypt with incredible power and authority. Potiphar's wife who lied on him, Potiphar who imprisoned him, the keepers of the prison who gave him his marching orders, and all who looked down on the Hebrew boy sold into Egypt saw him rise to unprecedented power. The new name Pharaoh gave him was "Zaphnath-paaneah" which means "Treasury of the glorious rest, or abundance of life." Who then would dare judge him by his scars or hold him hostage to his past? It is hard for the human mind to grasp such a dramatic shift that "came out of left field," as the saying goes. Imagine this moment as Joseph looked back at all he had been through and realized that maybe it was all part of God's divine plan. Think of how he would love to share the moment with his father, however, not knowing whether he was still alive. It would have been interesting to hear the conversations between Mr. and Mrs. Potiphar when they found themselves subjected to whatever Joseph decided for Egypt, especially when she recalled she lied about him and caused his imprisonment. In his wisdom, Solomon writes, "When a man's ways please the LORD, he maketh even his enemies to be at peace with him. Better is a little with righteousness than great revenues without right. A man's heart deviseth his way: But the LORD directeth his steps. A divine sentence is in the lips of the king: his mouth transgresseth not in judgment. A just weight and balance is the Lord's: all the weights of the bag are his work" (Proverbs 16: 11).

According to Genesis 37:2, Joseph was seventeen years old when he was sold into Egypt. He was thirty years old when he stood before Pharaoh. That means he spent thirteen years in pain, suffering, isolation, and abandonment before his change came. John, who escaped martyrdom, spent about thirteen years banished on the Isle of Patmos before the Lord sent him with letters to the seven churches in

Revelation. There are many thoughts concerning the number thirteen, some good and some bad. Whenever the number thirteen is referred to, it is generally negative. Someone says the number thirteen represents everything: Satan—for example, evil, wickedness, devils, and everything vile that is connected to them.

On the other hand, I tend to agree with another writer who sees thirteen as heralding that a change is coming. In looking at Joseph and John and many other examples in the Bible, one can say change is coming. It depends on whether your concept is that the glass is half full or half empty. I see it as half full. There are many other instances in the Bible where thirteen indicates a change is coming. Or something new has happened. In Joseph's case, it was more than change is coming. It was a fantastic turnaround that no one but God could see coming. If Joseph's scars were visible to the eyes, they would be something to behold.

The story concludes in an unscripted manner that baffles the mind. God, who knows the past and sees the future, devised a perfect plan for Israel's survival. It reminds me of the story of Esther, who became queen specifically for the times she was in and the things she would experience. Her cousin and mentor, Mordecai, believed that God would protect his people one way or the other. However, chances were that God allowed her to become queen with access to the king so that she could advocate for her people. "For if thou altogether holdest thy peace at this time, then shall there enlargement and deliverance arise to the Jews from another place; but thou and thy fathers house shall be destroyed: and who knoweth whether thou art come to the kingdom for such a time as this?" (Esther 4:14). One cannot see what God's plans are ahead of them coming to fruition. However, looking back and seeing how the pieces fall into place, he can say, God, you are awesome!

What are the chances other than the mighty hand of God working that the beloved son of Jacob is sold into Egypt and becomes the head of operations with complete control over wheat and grains when a severe famine is coming? Jacob knew not that Joseph was sold into Egypt. His brothers, who sold him, had no idea what had become of him. But God was about to bring it together, and the whole family finally realized God's inner workings. Famine took the land, and there was no grain or wheat except in Egypt. Jacob encouraged his sons to go down to Egypt to seek food so that they would survive. Strangely, Jacob refused to send Benjamin, Joseph's younger brother, with them. Those two last sons were of his old age, and he had lost Joseph (at least, that's what he was told). "But Benjamin, Joseph's brother, Jacob sent not with his brethren; for he said, Lest peradventure mischief befall him" (Genesis 42:4.)

When Joseph saw his brothers, he knew them, but they did not recognize him. Neither would they based on his position and authority. He has grown from a youth to an adult. He was sold into Egypt as a slave, and now he is the chief operating officer in Egypt, from the prison's dungeon to the high chair of the palace. He immediately remembered his dreams as he saw his brothers come to Egypt desperate for food and knew he had the power and authority to supply their needs. However, he noted that his younger brother was not there, and his father, if not dead, must be stricken in age.

Nevertheless, he intended to use a strategy on them to discover more about his little brother without revealing himself. On the one hand, there was the fulfillment of his dreams, while on the other hand, there are memories of the scars of hate and abandonment. Joseph's first strategy was to label them as spies to get them on the defensive. He knew they were not spies, but he was a man of great wisdom and was ready to put it to the test. He did not need confirmation of who they were, but in their desperation to prove they were not spies, they were willing to tell their whole story. "And they said, Thy servants are twelve brethren, the sons of one man in the land of Canaan; and, behold, the youngest is this day with our father, and one is not" (Genesis 42:13).

Note two things in that verse. One, they identified themselves as Joseph's servants. The word they used depicts an enslaved person or a bondman. That's why they hated him in the first place and eventually sold him into Egypt, which was less egregious than killing him. Two, they talked about the younger brother being with their father, but one was not. That word "not" implies one is not accounted for, or he was dead. There is a similar reference to the word in Matthew 2:18: "In Rama was there a voice heard, lamentation, and weeping, and great mourning, Rachel weeping for her children, and would not be comforted, because they are not." This cry happened after Herod had slain all the children two years and under in Bethlehem and the coasts around. The more his brothers spoke, the more information he received which gave him a sense of comfort that his younger brother and his father were okay. At the same time, Joseph had to do the hard things to see Benjamin. He jailed them for three days and continued to interrogate them while using it as a strategy for them to bring his younger brother.

In the sequence of these events, it became clear that the brothers had been worried about their actions that caused long-term pain in the family and a permanent loss of their brother. It is noticeable in their conversation that they felt they were being punished for what they had done to their brother, feeling that their lives were now in danger.

And they said one to another, We are verily guilty concerning our brother, in that we saw the anguish of his soul when he besought us, and we would not hear; therefore is this distress come upon us. And Reuben answered them, saying, Spake I not unto you, saying, Do not sin against the child; and ye would not hear? Therefore, behold, also his blood is required. And they knew not that Joseph understood them; for he spake unto them by an interpreter. And he turned himself about from them, and wept; and returned to them again, and communed with them, and took from them Simeon, and bound him before their eyes. (Genesis 42:21-24).

The guilt of conscience was obvious. The wicked flee when no man is running after him. It is reasonable to believe that they frequently spoke about their actions against Joseph, which was unjustified. Imagine Joseph listening to their confession in his presence, reliving the trauma while giving God thanks that his dreams were not a fantasy. If there were remaining questions in his mind, they were answered. Everyone was bearing the scars, and they would not realize it was for God's glory until the episode concluded. There were two theories about Joseph—one that his brothers knew and one that Jacob believed. The brothers knew they sold him to the Ishmaelites from Egypt, and Jacob believed wild animals killed him because that was the conspiracy. Now, Simeon is retained for security reasons or as collateral to guarantee they return with Benjamin. It is hard to wrap one's mind around the incredible work of God.

The step-by-step process that God allowed or created made it more complicated to grasp using the finite human mind to understand the infinite unrevealed things of God. Every step of the way, things were happening outside of the norm. For example, as angry and emotional as Joseph appeared behind the scenes, he advised his servants how to treat his brethren. They gave them all the goods they ordered and took their money but hid each person's amount they paid in their sacks. Under normal circumstances, they would be rejoicing. But how things unfolded, they had a mountain of reasons to fear. It could be a trick to implicate them in fraud or some other deceptive behavior. The dichotomy at work here could not be more unparalleled. Joseph used the strength of his power to intensify pressure on his brothers. They could not discover that he was using a double strategy against them. They ran into another hurdle whenever they thought they were free to go. Joseph's unrelenting plan was to get Benjamin to Egypt. On the other hand, there could be nothing worse for him to ask based on their knowledge of how Jacob would react.

Eventually, they were left without an option for Simeon's release; Judah agreed to bear the responsibility for Benjamin's safety and Simeon's freedom.

Genesis 43:8-14:
⁸ And Judah said unto Israel his father, Send the lad with me, and we will arise and go; that we may live, and not die, both we, and thou, and also our little ones. ⁹ I will be surety for him; of my hand shalt thou require him: if I bring him not unto thee, and set him before thee, then let me bear the blame for ever: ¹⁰ For except we had lingered, surely now we had returned this second time. ¹¹ And their father Israel said unto them, If it must be so now, do this; take of the best fruits in the land in your vessels, and carry down the man a present, a little balm, and a little honey, spices, and myrrh, nuts, and almonds: ¹² And take double money in your hand; and the money that was brought again in the mouth of your sacks, carry it again in your hand; peradventure it was an oversight: ¹³ Take also your brother, and arise, go again unto the man: ¹⁴ And God Almighty give you

mercy before the man, that he may send away your other brother, and Benjamin. If I be bereaved of my children, I am bereaved.

It would have been easy had Joseph called them by name and reminded them of what they had done to him. But that's not how God intended for it to go. The human mind may think of an immediate triumph and malicious reaction for self-gratification, but because it was the divine works of God in progress, Joseph followed the guidance of the Spirit as he was led to do. It is easy to look for the result without going through the process. Somehow, Joseph suppressed his emotions from being on public display. One can grasp from this that God will not give you an assignment without preparing you for it. In the process, he built character, patience, wisdom, and compassion under pressure. The tension was intense on all sides. No one was exempt from scars for God's glory. They brought Benjamin with them, gifts for (Joseph), the man they knew not who he was, and under the directions of Jacob, they brought back the money that was found in their sacks. All to appease the wrath of this mighty man in Egypt (oblivious that this powerful man was the brother they sold, although they saw terror in his eyes as they made the malicious decision) because of their desperation to survive the famine and not be held as bondmen. Joseph and his brothers were on two different tracks. His brothers were desperate for food and were overwhelmed with the fear of causing further hurt to their father by not having Simeon released and, worst of all, returning without Benjamin.

Contrary to their thinking, Joseph was on a track of discovery. With every step in the process, it appeared they were in deeper trouble and danger, while Joseph felt closer to closure with each step. After Judah's final plea and supplication, knowing that Jacob would not survive losing his last of two sons to Rachel, everything hung on him getting back in the arms and presence of his father. Here is the final dark hour of the night before the dawn broke. Here is Judah's final push to save his father's life.

Now therefore when I come to thy servant my father, and the lad be not with us; Seeing that his life is bound up in the lad's life; It shall come to pass, when he seeth that the lad is not with us, that he will die: and thy servants shall bring down the gray hairs of thy servant our father with sorrow to the grave. For thy servant became surety for the lad unto my father, saying, If I bring him not unto thee, then I shall bear the blame to my father for ever. Now therefore, I pray thee, let thy servant abide instead of the lad a bondman to my lord; and let the lad go up with his brethren. For how shall I go up to my father, and the lad be not with me? Lest peradventure I see the evil that shall come on my father (Genesis 44:30-34).

The conversation reached a breaking point for Joseph, who would love to see his father's open eyes again and not add further anguish to his past sixteen years. Finally, he could not hold his emotions any longer in disguise. He commanded that everyone be removed from the gathering to let him unveil his real identity to his brethren. All the emotions compacted in his heart like a combustion chamber came out like an eruption. "And he wept aloud: and the Egyptians and the house of Pharaoh heard. And Joseph said unto his brethren, I am Joseph; doth my father yet live? And his brethren could not answer him; for they were troubled at his presence" (Genesis 45:2-3). Imagine that their minds were moving fast forward and backward. They were already contemplating whether the experiences they were having were because of their heartless, hateful, and evil acts against Joseph. They realized he was not an enslaved person in Egypt and was not dead but had risen to unimaginable power. In such circumstances, a normal human reaction is to expect retaliation, especially when one has the power to do so.

Contrary to their way of thinking was Joseph's understanding that it was the Lord's doing in line with fulfilling his purpose. We have not been told in Scripture whether Joseph had more dreams about his time in Egypt and how God would use them for his glory. However, even without a specific dream, it was self-revelatory that the hand of God was deeply involved from the start. "And Joseph said unto his brethren, Come near to me, I pray you. And they came near. And he said, I am Joseph your brother, whom ye sold into Egypt" (V.4). Picture that in your mind what may be the various thoughts chroming through their minds. They had to wrestle with the possible consequences and their vulnerabilities. Benjamin was there and hearing for the first time that his brother had not died, as he was made to believe.

74

Then, they had to assess how they would unveil the truth to Jacob, which they kept sealed under pretense. The lies they told Jacob were vivid, graphic, and well-calculated. They dipped Joseph's coat in blood and stated that wild animals killed him. That means the coat was also destroyed to prove the aggression of such animal/s. That had been riveted in Jacob's mind, and he lived with a nightmare of imagination for a decade and a half. Taking ownership of Jacob, Joseph, and Benjamin's pain and suffering would not be easy, even ending with a successful story. But before their hearts were gripped with intense pain, Joseph had a word of consolation to help them see the bigger picture. I want to give you the chapter in perspective without altering it.

> *Genesis 45:5-28:*
> *⁵ Now therefore be not grieved, nor angry with yourselves, that ye sold me hither: for God did send me before you to preserve life. ⁶ For these two years hath the famine been in the land: and yet there are five years, in the which there shall neither be earing nor harvest. ⁷ And God sent me before you to preserve you a posterity in the earth, and to save your lives by a great deliverance. ⁸ So now it was not you that sent me hither, but God: and he hath made me a father to Pharaoh, and lord of all his house, and a ruler throughout all the land of Egypt. ⁹ Haste ye, and go up to my father, and say unto him, Thus saith thy son Joseph, God hath made me lord of all Egypt: come down unto me, tarry not: ¹⁰ And thou shalt dwell in the land of Goshen, and thou shalt be near*

unto me, thou, and thy children, and thy children's children, and thy flocks, and thy herds, and all that thou hast: ¹¹ *And there will I nourish thee; for yet there are five years of famine; lest thou, and thy household, and all that thou hast, come to poverty.* ¹² *And, behold, your eyes see, and the eyes of my brother Benjamin, that it is my mouth that speaketh unto you.* ¹³ *And ye shall tell my father of all my glory in Egypt, and of all that ye have seen; and ye shall haste and bring down my father hither.* ¹⁴ *And he fell upon his brother Benjamin's neck, and wept; and Benjamin wept upon his neck.* ¹⁵ *Moreover he kissed all his brethren, and wept upon them: and after that his brethren talked with him.* ¹⁶ *And the fame thereof was heard in Pharaoh's house, saying, Joseph's brethren are come: and it pleased Pharaoh well, and his servants.* ¹⁷ *And Pharaoh said unto Joseph, Say unto thy brethren, This do ye; lade your beasts, and go, get you unto the land of Canaan;* ¹⁸ *And take your father and your households, and come unto me: and I will give you the good of the land of Egypt, and ye shall eat the fat of the land.* ¹⁹ *Now thou art commanded, this do ye; take you wagons out of the land of Egypt for your little ones, and for your wives, and bring your father, and come.* ²⁰ *Also regard not your stuff; for the good of all the land of Egypt is yours.* ²¹ *And the children of Israel did so: and Joseph gave them wagons, according to the commandment of Pharaoh, and gave them provision for the way.* ²² *To all of them he gave each man changes of raiment; but to Benjamin he gave three hundred pieces of silver, and five changes of raiment. [23] And to his father he sent after this manner; ten asses laden with the good things of Egypt, and ten she asses laden with corn and bread and meat for his father by the way. [24] So he sent his brethren away, and they departed: and he said unto them, See that ye fall not out by the way. [25] And they went up out of Egypt, and came into the land of Canaan unto Jacob their father, [26] And told him, saying, Joseph is yet alive, and he is governor over all the land of Egypt. And Jacob's heart fainted, for he believed them not. [27] And they told him all the words of Joseph, which he had said unto them: and when he saw the wagons which Joseph had sent to carry him, the spirit of Jacob their father revived: [28] And Israel said, It is enough; Joseph my son is yet alive: I will go and see him before I die.*

A fascinating sequence of events occurred as Jacob decided to journey to Egypt. He left nothing in Canaan because he would not return. Jacob journeyed to Egypt and got to Beersheba, the southernmost part of the land of Canaan. Before entering Egypt, he stopped and offered sacrifice to the God of Isaac, his father. It is interesting because the record shows that Abraham and Isaac lived there for a while, according to Genesis 22:19 and 26:23. In chapter 21:33, Abraham planted a grove tree in Beersheba and called on the name of the Lord there. In Jacob's mind, it was his last opportunity to give thanks and honor to God as he departed the land that had such memorable significance to his family. It took Jacob a lot of courage and conviction to leave the land he was familiar with and move to a strange country. However, because it was God's plan for their lives, God spoke to him again, as he had done before, reassuring him that he would be with him as he made the journey. Here is another point of proof that the entire saga, the dramatic events, and the complicated stories of their lives were to fulfill God's purpose. "And God spake unto Israel in the visions of the night, and said, Jacob, Jacob. And he said, Here am I. And he said, I am God, the God of the father: fear not to go down into Egypt; for I will there make of thee a great nation: I will go down with thee into Egypt; and I will also surely bring thee up again; and Joseph shall put his hand upon thine eyes" (Genesis 46:2-4).

It catches my attention that God called him Jacob twice in verse 2, which seems to be a reminder of his previous encounter with him when he wrestled with the angel. What's the possible takeaway from that? God changed his name from Jacob to Israel when he was afraid to go south and encounter his brother Esau. It was an inflection point then, and here it was again. The same God who changed his name from Jacob to Israel and saved him from his brother's wrath was ready to journey with him to Egypt. Not only that, but God affirmed in his heart that he would see Joseph, and Joseph would put his hand upon his eyes. It was a great word of confirmation and consolation, one that Joseph was still alive, and two, he would care for him for the rest of his life. Immediately, he was sold on the move. What greater joy than to have God confirm that your journey will be safe, your sorrow will turn to joy, and there will be provision and protection for the rest of your life?

It may be rough on the journey, but if you receive a word of assurance from the Lord, run along despite how it looks. Without further hesitation, he was ready to go, and his sons were excited to take him to see the son long thought was dead. Pharaoh had already ordered wagons to take them on their journey to Egypt, and they gathered all their families, possessions, livestock, and goods and headed off to Egypt. "All the souls that came with Jacob into Egypt, which came out of his loins, besides Jacob's sons' wives. All the souls were threescore and six; And the sons of Joseph, which were born him in Egypt, were two souls: all the souls of the house of Jacob, which came into Egypt, were threescore and ten" (Genesis 46:26-27). Pharaoh commanded that Joseph direct his family to live in the land of Goshen, which he considered to be the best of the land of Egypt. As the Lord told Jacob, Joseph took great care of him and his family until the day he died. However, as time drew near for his departure, he called his favorite son, Joseph, and made a heartfelt request, maybe falling in line with what the Lord told him that he would bring him up from the land of Egypt. "And the time drew nigh that Israel must die; and he called his son Joseph, and said unto him, If now I have found grace n thy sight, put, I pray thee, thy hand under my thigh, and deal kindly and truly with me; bury me not, I pray thee, in Egypt: But I will lie with my fathers, and thou shalt carry me out of Egypt, and bury me in their burying place. And he said, I will do as thou hast said. And he said, Swear unto me. And he sware unto him. And Israel bowed himself upon the bed's head" (Genesis 47:29-31).

Jacob's life was filled with highs and lows but climaxed with a new sense of joy. The presence of Joseph was like therapy to him after he fell sick. He came to see him when his brothers told him his father was sick. When Israel heard that Joseph had come to see him, he strengthened himself and sat up on the bed. As he communed with his son, he reflected on God's promises to him. Israel recalled when God appeared to him at Luz in Canaan, blessed him, and told him he would make him fruitful and make a multitude of people out of him. Jacob also remembered that living in the land of Canaan was an everlasting covenant for all his generation. Hence, he did not want his body to remain in Egypt. How many things can go upside down in the sight of man while in God's doing; they are perfect in his design? There is no accurate answer to that question because God refuses to be boxed into any protocol designed by man. He will stick to his declaration because he cannot turn his back away from his word.

God changes customs and traditions when they do not fit his agenda. Something strange might be overlooked here because the focus is generally on Jacob and Joseph. Israel took ownership of Joseph's two sons, whom he had just gotten a chance to meet. He decided not to leave them from being under the umbrella and covering of the God of Abraham, Isaac, and Jacob. All that Israel knew, or was made to believe, was that Joseph was dead. Therefore, it was an overwhelming joy to know that Joseph was alive. Then, to see him face-to-face was unimaginable. To cap the whole thing off, he realized that Joseph also had two sons, who were born in Egypt and were not covered under the blessings of Israel. "And Israel beheld Joseph's sons, and said, Who are these? And Joseph said unto his father, They are my sons, whom God had given me in this place. And he said, Bring them, I pray thee, unto me, and I will bless them" (Genesis 48:9). At this juncture in the life of Jacob, his eyes had gotten dim, and he could not see clearly.

Nevertheless, Israel wanted to bless Joseph and his two sons. As he brought them to him, he began to reflect on the previous years in which he resolved in his mind that Joseph had died a brutal death. In verse 11, he said, "I had not thought to see thy face: and, lo, God hath shewed me also thy seed." As Joseph brought his sons to his father so that he could pronounce the blessings on them, it is conceivable that his mind was on history in making sure the blessings went according to protocol. One could see that in the presentation of his sons to his father. Joseph was deliberate as he held both sons in his arms at the same time. Manasseh was the elder, and Ephraim was the younger. In facing his father, he held Manasseh in his left hand and Ephraim in his right hand. The reason, one concludes, was making it easier for Israel not to miss the older son as he raised his right hand to bless them.

What happened next was beyond Joseph's comprehension. He watched curiously as Israel crossed his hands from left to right, placing his right hand on the head of Ephraim and his left hand on the head of Manasseh. It's important to remember that Israel's eyes were getting dim, and because of that, the first thing one can imagine is that Joseph thought that was why his father missed the firstborn child, who, by tradition, should receive the blessing. Note what is written in the text. "And Israel stretched out his right hand, and laid it upon Ephraim's head, who was the younger, and his left hand upon Manasseh's head, guiding his hands wittingly; for Manasseh was the firstborn" (v.14). Then Israel blessed Joseph and while reflecting on the goodness, mercy, and grace of God who had been faithful to his fathers, Abraham and Isaac, and the angel who redeemed him from evil all his life until that day. How can one forget Jacob's life, journey, and experiences? At that moment (one can conclude), he looked back at his life despite all the pains and scars he bore to fulfill God's purpose and expressed gratitude to God. In retrospect, Romans 8:28 was fulfilled in the life of Israel. "And we know that all things work together for good to them that love God, to them who are the called according to his purpose." The same source of his blessings, guidance, and protection he passed on to Joseph and his two sons. He was extending some of the exact words that were said to him to his son and grandsons. It was okay with Joseph until he realized that the blessings of the firstborn were being bestowed on Ephraim.

And when Joseph saw that his father laid his right hand upon the head of Ephraim, it displeased him: and he held up his father's hand, to remove it from Ephraim's head unto Manasseh's head. And Joseph said unto his father, Not so, my father: for this is the firstborn; put thy right hand upon his head. And his father refused, and said, I know it, my son, I know it: he also shall become a people, and he also shall be great: but truly his younger brother shall be greater than he, and his seed shall become a multitude of nations. (Genesis 48:17-19)

It was surprising and disappointing to Joseph, but when he realized that his father had not made a mistake, he had no choice but to accept the doings of the Lord. The irony is that Jacob's life took the same path, although the beginning was different. His journey began through deception, while Ephraim's blessing came under divine unction. His encouragement to Joseph was that the Lord would bless him and eventually cause him to return to the land of his fathers. Such fulfillment would occur centuries later, but God's promises remained true. Finally, Israel called all his sons together and declared to each of them what their future would be like, good or bad. One cannot but note the prophetic declaration to Judah despite his mistakes and downfalls. Being in line as part of God's plan of the scarlet thread of redemption does not make one spotless and without blemish. That truth was evident in Judah's life. Nevertheless, of the twelve tribes of Israel, Judah's tribe was the Messianic tribe, and Israel made it known to him that his brethren would praise him and bow down before him.

It is strange that for unknown reasons, Joseph's brothers never appear confident that their transgressions were forgiven. They seemed comfortable while Jacob was alive because of the excitement of the reunion between him and Joseph. However, the scars of conscience are hard to remove; they have been displayed among the brothers since they went to Egypt to buy wheat, and how uncertain all of them were whether they would be called spies or accused of wrongdoing. Because of their awareness of how Joseph was treated, the brothers contemplated whether their experiences were ramifications of their actions. Israel's request to be buried among his fathers, and after his passing, his request was granted. "And when Joseph's brethren saw that their father was dead, they said, Joseph will peradventure hate us, and will certainly requite us all the evil which we did unto him" (Genesis 50:15). The understanding of God's plan and purpose was not made known to them. All they could think of was the injustice they had done to their brother and the terror that was in his eyes when they sold him to the Egyptians.

Normal human reactions anticipate retaliation. They sent messengers to Joseph using their father's name to bring them covering and protection from Joseph's retribution. "And they sent a messenger unto Joseph, saying, Thy father did command before he died, saying, So shall ye say unto Joseph, Forgive, I pray thee now, the trespass of thy brethren, and their sin; for they did unto thee evil: and now, we pray thee, forgive the trespass of the servants of the God of thy father. And Joseph wept when they spake unto him" (V.16-17). No one knows where this story came from. It appeared to be made up because of fear. Of all the things Jacob told Joseph in his final days, he did not mention that in the conversation while stating the remainder of their lives. They put their survival and mercy under the name of their dead father, who was not able to speak for himself. However, the thinking ought to be that Joseph would honor his father's words and spare their lives. A guilty conscience follows you wherever you go. And as we read in Proverbs 28:1, "The wicked flee when no man pursueth: but the righteous are bold as a lion." All his brothers except Benjamin felt their survival was at Joseph's mercy, and the unceasing remorse and confession were to their benefit. Not only did they use their father's name, but they also fell on their faces before him and offered to be his servants. Remember, they resisted the very thought of Joseph's dreams that they would fall obeisance to him, but now, desperate to spare their lives, it was easy to do as they observed the power Joseph had. His brothers lied to Jacob about Joseph, telling him that he died, and now they are lying to Joseph after their father died. Little did they know that the scars and pains of the family were for God's glory, but the natural mind could not comprehend that.

Eventually, they were brought into the light as Joseph disclosed that God was at work in the process. So, to set their hearts at ease, he said, "Fear not: for am I in the place of

God?" In other words, Joseph was telling them that if there will be retribution against you, God will find a way to do it, but he was not inclined to do so. "But as for you," he said, "Ye thought evil against me; but God meant it for good, to bring to pass, as it is this day, to save much people alive. Now therefore fear ye not: I will nourish you, and your little ones. And he comforted them, and spake kindly unto them" (Vs. 19-21). Generations later, as Joseph came to the end of his days, he reiterated what his father had said concerning the promises of God to their fathers, Abraham, Isaac, and Jacob. "And Joseph said unto his brethren, I die: and God will surely visit you, and bring you out of this land unto the land which he sware to Abraham, Isaac, and to Jacob. And Joseph took an oath of the children of Israel, saying, God will surely visit you, and ye shall carry up my bones from hence" (Vs.24-25). Shortly after, Joseph died at one hundred and ten years old. They embalmed his body and placed it in a coffin. That was the end of his time in Egypt, but he fulfilled all that God desired of him, allowing him to be sold in Egypt as an enslaved person. Although God's promises did not come to fruition until centuries later, they were authentic, and eventually, they made it out of Egypt and carried the bones of Joseph with them. We can all learn from those experiences that God's will does not always come easy or fit in the systematic configuration of one's mind.

The story is long, but it is one of the most fascinating stories of the Bible. There have been scars left, right, and center from the beginning. Just recap for a moment. "Scarred for God's glory" is one of the most incredible depictions one can look at. There is no warning to Jacob as it was given to Saul concerning the things he would suffer for the cause of Christ and the testimony of a changed life. Only a few things went well in the life of this patriarch that one can celebrate by looking at it from a face value.

Would you associate God with what Rebecca did to rob Esau of his birthright? In the eyes of righteousness, can you see God working in the deception of Isaac? Because of his blindness and old age, he blessed the second son and not the son who was strategically positioned for such a blessing. In your assessment, do you conclude that Esau was right in wanting to kill Jacob for depriving him of what belonged to him? Looking forward at Jacob's life, one sees nothing but him facing the consequences of his bad behavior. What are the possibilities of considering his life's ups and downs as a reward for selfish acts? One would be hard-pressed to see how all these crooked and unbecoming of righteousness ways could have a place in the divine plans of God. Frequently, it must have run through his mind that his life would not be as complicated as it was if he had done justly to his brother. How about giving him children through wives and concubines until he reached God's pre-determined number of twelve sons? What had been considered a blessing spiraled into a curse. The welcome that God opened the womb of Rachel and blessed him with a son in old age— and what started as the highest level of celebration became the most profound depth of anguish and pain.

After many years of hiding and isolation living in the north, Jacob was ready to go south with a large family and great wealth. However, riveted in the recesses of his mind was his broken relationship with his brother Esau, and believing that although the time had been so long, he was still in grave danger in facing the wrath of his brother. Desperate to find hope, peace, and safety, he desired God's intervention. He did all he could that was humanly possible to provide compensation to his brother with the hope of reconciliation, but the doubts were rooted in his psyche. If you do not know the story, here is a portion of Scripture to give you a view of the context.

> *Genesis 32:9-32*
> *⁹ And Jacob said, O God of my father Abraham, and God of my father Isaac, the LORD which saidst unto me, Return unto thy country, and to thy kindred, and I will deal well with thee: ¹⁰ I am not worthy of the least of all the mercies, and of all the truth, which thou hast shewed unto thy servant; for with my staff I passed over this Jordan; and now I am become two bands. ¹¹ Deliver me, I pray thee, from the hand of my brother, from the hand of Esau: for I fear him, lest he will come and smite me, and the mother with the children. ¹² And thou saidst, I will surely do thee good, and make thy seed as the sand of the sea, which cannot be numbered for multitude. ¹³ And he lodged there that same night; and took of that which came to his hand a present for Esau his brother; ¹⁴ Two hundred she goats, and twenty he goats, two hundred*

ewes, and twenty rams, ¹⁵ Thirty milch camels with their colts, forty kine, and ten bulls, twenty she asses, and ten foals. ¹⁶ And he delivered them into the hand of his servants, every drove by themselves; and said unto his servants, Pass over before me, and put a space betwixt drove and drove. ¹⁷ And he commanded the foremost, saying, When Esau my brother meeteth thee, and asketh thee, saying, Whose art thou? And whither goest thou? And whose are these before thee? ¹⁸ Then thou shalt say, They be thy servant Jacob's; it is a present sent unto my lord Esau: and, behold, also he is behind us. ¹⁹ And so commanded he the second, and the third, and all that followed the droves, saying, On this manner shall ye speak unto Esau, when ye find him. ²⁰ And say ye moreover, Behold, thy servant Jacob is behind us. For he said, I will appease him with the present that goeth before me, and afterward I will see his face; peradventure he will accept of me. ²¹ So went the present over before him: and himself lodged that night in the company. ²² And he rose up that night, and took his two wives, and his two womenservants, and his eleven sons, and passed over the ford Jabbok. ²³ And he took them, and sent them over the brook, and sent over that he had. ²⁴ And Jacob was left alone; and there wrestled a man with him until the breaking of the day. ²⁵ And when he saw that he prevailed not against him, he touched the hollow of his thigh; and the hollow of Jacob's thigh was out of joint, as he wrestled with him. ²⁶ And he said, Let me go, for the *day breaketh. And he said, I will not let thee go, except thou bless me. ²⁷ And he said unto him, What is thy name? And he said, Jacob. ²⁸ And he said, Thy name shall be called no more Jacob, but Israel: for as a prince hast thou power with God and with men, and hast prevailed. ²⁹ And Jacob asked him, and said, Tell me, I pray thee, thy name. And he said, Wherefore is it that thou dost ask after my name? And he blessed him there. ³⁰ And Jacob called the name of the place Peniel: for I have seen God face to face, and my life is preserved. ³¹ And as he passed over Penuel the sun rose upon him, and he halted upon his thigh. ³² Therefore the children of Israel eat not of the sinew which shrank, which is upon the hollow of the thigh, unto this day: because he touched the hollow of Jacob's thigh in the sinew that shrank.*

After all, he had an encounter with the Lord in the form of an angel, and somehow, that unique experience made him believe this was his moment if his life would be turned around. He didn't squander it. Despite the physical cost, he felt nothing else could help. Even then, with his new name (Israel; He will rule as God) from his old name (Jacob, a heel catcher or a supplanter) and his declaration of seeing God face-to-face, the trajectory of his life did not change for the better. Although Esau did not kill him because of God's purpose in his life, it got worse.

Suddenly, the treasured son of Jacob's old age with dreams and visions was sold into Egypt but believed to be dead for as much as Jacob was made to believe. Then unbearable famine took the land, and Egypt was the only place where wheat was available, preserved by the wisdom of Joseph and credit to God because Joseph told Pharaoh that only God could interpret his dreams. How much can one man bear for the glory of God? We cannot ask Jacob, Joseph, and the entire family, but that's why God had the story enacted and written down for our learning. Therefore, never judge or predetermine the will of God based on how a process works. Over and over again, we see the difficulties and struggles of the people whom God used to accomplish great things. If you fall in that category, be patient and allow God's sustaining grace and wisdom to guide you to your destiny.

The experiences of people being scarred for God's glory are not only found in the Old Testament but also in the New Testament. The same is true for you and me in this dispensation of grace. God has given them as examples for us to learn from and build confidence in his wisdom and power to bring us through victoriously.

CHAPTER SIX

PAUL, SCARRED FOR GOD'S GLORY

When the Lord called Saul, he chose him despite his character scars. He had a reputation for torture, abuse, and imprisonment of Christians. It started at a young age, and Saul was there and witnessed the stoning of Stephen, one of the first ordained deacons of the church. His life was focused on causing suffering, death, and the imprisonment of Christians, which he was not afraid to explain in Acts 22. Paul testified of the transforming experience that changed his life forever. The first account is recorded in Acts 9 and recalled in chapter 22, where he made it clear that he did not believe he was worthy of the call. Here is part of his account: "And I said, Lord, they know that I imprisoned and beat in every synagogue them that believed on thee: And when the blood of thy martyr Stephen was shed, I also was standing by, and consenting unto his death, and kept the raiment of them that slew him" (Acts 22:19-20). His history of evil was widespread among the followers of Christ, and they were afraid of him, though he confessed about his past and declared his conversion.

93

Ananias was not impressed even though he was listening to the voice of God. His immediate rejection of Saul proves he was unwilling to look beyond what he knew of his past. However, the Lord's response was quick and assertive. "Go thy way: for he is a chosen vessel unto me, to bear my name before the Gentiles, and kings, and the children of Israel" Acts 9:15. Saul had character scars, but his assignment for the Lord would cause him emotional and physical wounds. Unsurprisingly, he wrote about his suffering later in life, fulfilling what Christ predicted would happen. Here is what the Lord said to Ananias, "For I will show him how great things he must suffer for my name's sake" Acts 9:16. All through the life of Saul, who became Paul, he suffered for the cause of Christ, and his testimony of God's grace. He sustained the scars attributed to a betrayer. They ridiculed him, beat him, imprisoned him, and eventually, they crucified him for his testimony about his newfound faith. Listen to his words.

Are they ministers of Christ? (I speak as a fool.) I am more; in labours more abundant, in stripes above measure, in prisons more frequent, in deaths oft. Of the Jews, five times received I forty stripes save one. Thrice was I beaten with rods, once was I stoned, thrice I suffered shipwreck, a night and a day I have been in the deep; In journeyings often, in perils of waters, in perils of robbers, in perils by mine own countrymen, in perils by the heathen, in perils in the city, in perils in the wilderness, in perils in the sea, in perils among false brethren; In weariness and painfulness, in watchings often, in hunger and thirst, in fastings often, in cold and nakedness. (2 Corinthians 11:23-27)

That is a summary of the apostle's testimony of what he experienced for his testimony of Christ. Note (in case you are having problems with members of your church or household): Paul made it clear that he suffered perils among false brethren and the Jews, his blood brothers. In case you missed it in the text, numerous times, he was beaten with rods and striped numerous times. Stripes in those days usually left severe marks and sometimes deep wounds. His conclusion in Galatians 6:17, "From henceforth let no man trouble me: for I bear in my body the marks of the Lord Jesus."

The Greek word Paul used for "marks" is transliterated as "stigma." When Paul used that word to describe his experiences, he used a word commonly understood as an enslaved person or soldier bearing the stamp or mark of his master. Strong's Definition is "To stick, that is to prick. A mark incised or punched (for recognition of ownership), figuratively, a scar for service." The point of emphasis is that the scars we carry for the cause of Christ are worth everything we go through. Likewise, if God has healed you of your scars and from them, hold your head high and rejoice in him despite what others think, believe, or do.

The experience revolutionized his life and radicalized him to push harder for the kingdom of God, hoping that his determination and pride would impact the lives of others. Paul was never ashamed of the scars he received for his relationship with Christ. He was never afraid to be scarred further as he defended his new life. He made it clear that he was not ashamed of the gospel of Christ because it was the power of God unto salvation.

Scars, sometimes, are for God's glory. Although God gave Paul a glimpse into the third heaven and showed him amazing things that he said were unlawful to mention, he allowed him to undergo severe tests to keep him humble.

These are some of the words he penned about his experience.

And lest I should be exalted above measure through the abundance of the revelations, there was given to me a thorn in the flesh, the messenger of Satan to buffet me, lest I should be exalted above measure. For this thing I besought the Lord thrice, that it might depart from me. And he said unto me, 'My grace is sufficient for thee: for my strength is made perfect in weakness.' Most gladly therefore will I rather glory in my infirmities, that the power of Christ may rest upon me.

Therefore, I take pleasure in infirmities, in reproaches, in necessities, in persecutions, in distresses for Christ's sake: for when I am weak, then am I strong, 2 Corinthians 12:7-10 (KJV).

There are many speculations about the apostle's statement in this passage. Some conclude that the infirmity he spoke about had to do with his sight, sighting his statement in Galatians 6:11, "Ye see how large a letter I have written unto you with mine own hand." He was not referring to the font size but the letter's length. He had personally written this letter compared to other times when he dictated and others wrote. Let us see what his expression suggests. The critical statements in the text are, "There was given to me a thorn in the flesh" and "the messenger of Satan to buffet me." And what was the thorn in his description?

The word messenger comes from the Greek "Aggelos" and is pronounced "Angelos," meaning angel. That means an angel of Satan constantly "buffets" him. What does the word buffet, "Kolaphizo," mean? It is to cuff, to give a box on the face. We see the same word used in Jesus' trial before the high priest in Matthew 26:67: "Then did they spit in his face and buffeted him; others smote him with the palms of their hands." The word means to "rap with the fist." Thayer's Definition says, "To strike with the fist, to give one a blow with the fist, to maltreat, or to treat with violence."

I have also seen the word expressed as constantly hitting at the same place. Suffice it to say if you keep hitting one with a fist, that person will suffer bruises and scars. There was nothing artificial or superficial about his experience, but wounds are sometimes for God's glory. The Lord's response to his request affirms it. He did not promise to hinder the devil from bruising him, but he promised to give him the needed grace to sustain him during the test. Chances you have been struggling with similar experiences or something different but have been asking the Lord for relief and have not gotten it. Maybe you have been praying for a long time and wondering why things have not changed. It is possible that you have told the Lord time and again that you cannot handle it anymore. Often, what we have pre-conceived God should do is far from what he intends for us or how he plans to get us through. Chances are you are being scarred for God's glory or your benefit, and God is continuing to supply and sustain you with his grace to prevent you from crumbling under the burden or stress of the situation.

The average person who trusts God's judgment and wisdom and gives him control of his life will be patient if he knows what he is experiencing is for God's glory. The problem is that we keep speaking and do not take the time to listen. If we pause and listen to what the Lord is saying, we might hear him say what he said to the apostle Paul. "My grace is sufficient for thee: for my strength is made perfect in weakness." Having realized that God's response was not to remove his infirmity but to keep him victorious through the sustenance of grace, he replied, "Most gladly therefore will I rather glory in my infirmities, that the power of Christ may rest upon me" (2 Corinthians 12:9). What would your response be if you know that you were scarred for God's glory, or that the things you are experiencing are allowed by the Lord for your benefit? How would you respond to critics or skeptics who are willing to judge you or pass assertions against you in their ignorance? Would you have the courage and boldness to come to the same conclusion as Paul? "Therefore I take pleasure in infirmities, in reproaches, in necessities, in persecutions, in distresses for Christ's sake: for when I am weak, then am I strong" (Verse 10).

Here is what one can take solace in. If your life has been scarred, you had a checkered past before the Lord called you, or if you have had bad experiences after he called you, he knew your history, destiny, and the journey you must travel to get there. Yet he chose you for those possible reasons. Imagine, the man the Gentiles feared the most was the man God called to be his mouthpiece to them. How great is the irony? I do not believe that Paul had a self-esteem problem; however, I do believe that his conscience constantly reminded him of his history.

Jacob is another person in the Bible whose life was scarred.

CHAPTER SEVEN

JACOB AND THE CONSPIRACY THEORY

Anyone without a past has not lived a day on this earth. Man inevitably makes mistakes. It is impossible to live in the fallen nature of Adam and not have unfortunate experiences. It is hard to find a man or woman that God has used who did not have things happen they wish didn't, whether before being called or during the process of being used by him. It's easy to look at the story of Jacob from the point of deception and lambast him for being dishonest, grudgeful, conniving, and a betrayer. How would you judge Jacob's life? His life has been filled with deception, from the conspiracy of Rebekah to robbing Esau of his birthright. You can read the story in Genesis 27-29.

At the beginning of this saga that shaped Jacob's life, no one will give Rebekah credit or stand with Jacob for their conspiracy to deprive Esau of what was rightfully his according to traditions and customs. What would one say if God whispered and said, that's exactly how I want it to play out? Would you call him deceptive and conniving? The

101

beauty of God's plan doesn't always start in the manner man approves. Isaac blessed Jacob, although he had doubts. However, the blessing was not reversible. You need to bear that in mind as well. It is not dependent on others' approval because God never makes mistakes. However, your mistakes are often designed to fulfill God's purpose, and those who do not understand will voice their disapproval. God is the one who will take you through the dark places of your journey and the difficult times in your life.

As much as Isaac was frustrated, the norm had been broken, and he realized he could not withdraw his blessings from Jacob. Now, he decided to instruct him as a father and remind him of God's promises to Abraham. Painfully, he blessed him with the biologically ancestral blessing and posterity and now realized he had to pronounce on him the blessings of God's promise as was required. "And Isaac called Jacob, and blessed him, and charged him, and said unto him, thou shalt not take a wife of the daughters of Canaan. Arise, go to Padanaram, to the house of Bethuel thy mother's father; and take thee a wife from thence of the daughters of Laban thy mother's brother" (This was not all he had to say to him at this crucial time in his life, but he continued to say) "And God Almighty bless thee, and make thee fruitful, and multiply thee, that thou mayest be a multitude of people; and give thee the blessing of Abraham, to thee, and to thy seed with thee; that thou mayest inherit the land wherein thou are a stranger, which God gave unto Abraham" (Genesis 28:1-4).

I mention this because Jacob's life did not shine for God's glory following these blessings. His life was more than checkered from here. However, he was still in God's plan to be the progenitor of the lineage from whom the Messiah would come. Don't judge me by my scars! Read the full story in Genesis if you have not yet done so. As you read, you may see yourself in the same or similar situations, and people may reject and despise you, but in all of your struggles, if God's purpose is in your life, it will come to fruition despite your past and scars. The mess got even closer to the Messiah with Judah, the fourth son of Jacob, who disgraced himself after accusing his daughter-in-law Tamar of prostitution and realized he was the father of the twins she bore. Judah had three sons: Er, Onan, and Shelah. Er married Tamar, and because of his sinful lifestyle, he died. His second brother, Onan, second in line, should carry on his brother's lineage by marrying his wife. However, because of personal grudges, he refused to impregnate Tamar. Because of that, he was killed for breaking the tradition as the Lord intended. Because of the death of the other two brothers, Judah appeared afraid to allow her to marry Shelah, so he shielded him from her.

Judah required Tamar to remain a widow until Shelah was grown. However, the time elapsed, and that plan never materialized. Eventually, Judah's wife, Shuah, died, and he was comforted by his sheepshearers and other friends. He went to spend time with his friends and, in the process, to shear sheep. Tamar struggled with losing two husbands (while remaining a widow) but still held the right to produce the seed of her first husband. "And it was told Tamar, saying, Behold thy father-in-law goeth up to Timnath to shear his sheep. And she put her widow's garments off from her, and covered her with a veil, and wrapped herself, and sat in an open place, which is by the way to Timnath; for she saw that Shelah was grown, and she was not given unto him to wife" (Genesis 38:13-14). When analyzing this story, there are two things to consider: judging me by my scars and holding me hostage to my past. Tamar did wrong, but Judah did worse. One can conclude that Tamar knew of Judah's character and felt she could trap him. Tamar set the bait, and he did bite. She dressed as a prostitute and positioned herself where he would see her. Nothing could be taken for granted, so there was a contingency plan. In the case that she conceived, there was no doubt it would anger Judah, and she would be reprimanded and punished. The holier-than-thou attitude would manifest itself without hesitation.

"When Judah saw her, he thought her to be a harlot, because she had covered her face. And he turned unto her by the way, and said, Go to, I pray thee, let me come in unto thee; (for he knew not that she was his daughter-in-law). And she said, what wilt thou give me, that thou mayest come in unto me?" When asked what he would give for the experience, he pledged a kid from the flock. A kid from the flock would not suffice. Tamar wanted something he could not deny ownership of. That was the only way she could pin him down as the father of her children. To his surprise and demise, his daughter-in-law, dressed like a prostitute, knew what could hold him accountable. "And he said, What pledge shall I give thee? And she said, Thy signet, and thy bracelets, and thy staff that is in thine hand. And he gave her, and came in unto her, and she conceived by him." Those gadgets would become invaluable to her. The price a man would pay for a moment with a woman is incredible. If he had planned to deceive her with a false promise of a kid, he found himself on the losing side. When his servants came to find her, she was nowhere to be found. However, she held on to those precious valuables until the time was right.

Some might disagree with me that God would have it that she conceived. However, divine providence dictates how God's plans will be executed, whether man approves or disapproves. I can imagine how Judah was haunted that he had lost his valuables but could not sound an alarm because of how they were lost because he was ashamed. Three months later, the news spread that Tamar was pregnant; she was in danger of death for playing the harlot. Oops, danger lurks! "And it came to pass about three months after, that it was told Judah, saying, Tamar, thy daughter-in-law hath played the harlot; and also, behold, she is with child by whoredom. And Judah said, Bring her forth, and let her be burnt" (Genesis 38:24). He that hath no sin, let him cast the first stone, or let him kindle the fire. Please think of her joy for having conceived the child by Judah and having his staff, signet, and bracelets in her position. She was confident that her life would be protected after the disclosure, and her dream would become a reality. Tamar was happy to be brought to Judah. To his astonishment, he was the one who impregnated her. Don't judge me by my scars because you have scars as well. You do not need to show someone how wrong they are to prove how right you are. No one is perfect, no, not one!

Joyfully, "When she was brought forth, she sent to her father-in-law, saying, By the man, whose these are, am I with child: and she said, Discern, I pray thee, whose are these, the signet, the bracelets, and staff. And Judah acknowledged them, and said, She hath been more righteous than I; because that I gave her not Shelah, my son." We have seen many examples of people who are quick to condemn others until it is discovered that they are no better and sometimes worse. In the combination of human failure and the desire to gratify the craving for the flesh is the plan of God being fulfilled. The average person would not write a script like that because it does not represent moral values, and one would not want his name attached to that sequence of events. However, God is not afraid to use the base things of the earth to fulfill his purpose and confound the wise and the holier than thou.

Despite the turmoil and chaos, Judah was God's elect from whom would come the Lord's Christ, the Messiah. Not only was Judah chosen to be a lion's whelp, but from him came the Lion of the Tribe of Judah. In case you have not read the story, this encounter with Tamar from which she conceived twin sons, one of those sons, was the lineage from which Christ came. With all that unfolds in this sequence of events, who could imagine God bringing the Savior of the world out of it? Many dark moments we experience are intended to shine God's light in those dark places to convince the world of his power to bring change.

Let's remind ourselves that God does not follow human guidelines and is not obligated to fit in the mold of man's approval. The Lord made it clear to Isaiah, "For my thoughts are not your thoughts, neither are your ways my ways, saith the LORD. For as the heavens are higher than the earth, so are my ways higher than your ways, and my thoughts than your thoughts" (Isaiah 55:8-9).

The same was made clear to Samuel when he was sent to Jessie's house to anoint a king. After Jessie thought he had exhausted bringing forth his sons, he was convinced none fit the criteria God was looking for. But the Lord told Samuel that he should not go by sight alone. "But the LORD said unto Samuel, look not on his countenance, or on the height of his stature; because I have refused him: for the LORD seeth not as man seeth; for man looketh at the outward appearance, but the LORD looketh on the heart" (1 Samuel 16:7).

Let it be known to those inclined to use your history as a prologue to your future that God does not look through the eyes of men. Imagine if he did; there would be no one for us to use as an example when we stumble and fall or find ourselves with unintended scars.

CHAPTER EIGHT

THE SCARS OF CONSCIENCE

The scars of conscience are the most difficult to get rid of. They are rooted deep in the fiber of one's heart and are undiscoverable by others. However, they could negatively affect one's life and alter one's ability to move forward. Merriam-Webster describes conscience as "The sense or consciousness of the moral goodness or blameworthiness of one's own conduct, intentions, or character together with a feeling of obligation to do right or be good." The Bible also describes conscience as a moral consciousness. Did you know that the word conscience had not appeared in the Old Testament, although we see its operation manifested many times? God gave a man a conscience to make him conscious of what he does wrong and brings conviction for him to make wrongs right.

Ironically, the first appearance of conscience in the Bible is found in John 8:9 when the men brought the woman to Jesus, who was said to be caught in adultery. John gives us an insight into the event as it took place. He tells us how the ulterior motive of the men was to test or tempt Jesus to see if he would uphold or break Moses' law. But Jesus, the Omniscient One who knew them from within, decided to test their consciences as he wrote: "He that is without sin among you, let him first cast a stone. And again he stooped down, and wrote on the ground." Here is the key verse, "And they which heard it, being convicted by their own conscience, went out one by one, beginning at the eldest, even unto the last: and Jesus was left alone, and the woman standing in the midst" (John 8:7-9).

Never underestimate the power of conscience. However, God has not given us a conscience to hold ourselves hostage but to create an awareness of wrongs, avoid them, or make wrongs right when we do them. In the wisdom of Solomon, he wrote, "The wicked flee when no one pursues, but the righteous are bold as a lion" (Proverbs 28:1). We see the working of conscience in the beginning with Adam and Eve who disobeyed God's direction and were afraid to meet him at the familiar meeting place. Instead, they went hiding. The second dispensation was the dispensation of conscience following the dispensation of innocence. When one looks at David's prayer in Psalm 51, it is a cry of desperation coming from a deep place of consciousness triggered by a guilty conscience. What David did was publicly known. However, being king made him unanswerable to man. Nevertheless, the feeling of separation from God caused by his moral decline took a stranglehold on him. Observing his prayer, one sees conviction, remorse, acknowledgment, brokenness, repentance, the fear of abandonment, and an earnest cry for renewal and restoration.

Scars of the conscience are often known only by God and the individual. However, that does not make it easier to deal with. The devil also tries to play psychological war games in our heads (hearts). He desires to keep us on edge and question whether God has forgiven us. As a result, he keeps us constantly looking over our proverbial shoulders. Whenever that happens, we believe others know about us. If a discussion arises concerning what worries our conscience, we take ownership and continue to re-live our past. What, then, does it take to feel relief and freedom from the scars of the conscience? Let's look back at David's approach in Psalm 51. He declared that God does not desire sacrifice; hence, he would give it. However, he knew what God desired and how he would be relieved of his past. "The sacrifices of God are a broken spirit: a broken and contrite heart, O God, thou wilt not despise" verse 16.

How does one get past the hurdle of a scarred conscience? He must have faith in the promises of God and accept his word to be true. It must become an act of faith in God's word through which justification comes. The apostle said to the Hebrews in 11:6, "But without faith, it is impossible to please him: for he that cometh to God must believe that he is, and that he is a rewarder of them that diligently seek him." Another thing to remember is that God is faithful in his promises, and through the voice of the apostle Paul, we are admonished to come boldly to the throne of grace, where we will find mercy and grace to help every time we need it. Sins are not forgiven when a heart is not penitent, but, on the other hand, sins will be permanently removed from every heart that truly repents. Finally, once God has forgiven you, he will never rehash it or them.

I have said this repeatedly and will continue to say it. One of my favorite portions of Scripture is found in Romans 5:19-21. "For as by one man's disobedience many were made sinners, so by the obedience of one shall many be made righteous. Moreover, the law entered that the offence might abound. But where sin abounded, grace did much more abound: That as sin hath reigned unto death, even so, might grace reign through righteousness unto eternal life by Jesus Christ our Lord." When God has forgiven you, forgive yourself and walk in his freedom.

CHAPTER NINE

THE PURPOSE OF GRACE

The purpose of redeeming grace is to turn one's life around and move you past your past. Here is an excellent example of what it means to have a changed life by the redemptive blood of Jesus Christ, which changes your status and position in Christ. Paul highlighted the life history of the Corinthians and brought to their attention those who will not make it into the kingdom of God. "Be not deceived," he said, "Neither fornicators, nor idolaters, nor adulterers, nor effeminate, nor abusers of themselves with mankind, nor thieves, nor covetous, nor drunkards, nor revilers, nor extortioners, shall inherit the kingdom of God" (1 Corinthians 6:9-10). However, the apostle did not identify the sins that would disqualify one from entering the kingdom, leaving them feeling condemned and lost. He reminded them that God had moved them from their past. In verse 11, he writes, "And such were some of you: but ye are washed, but ye are sanctified, but ye are justified in the name of the Lord Jesus, and by the Spirit of our God." That's the reassurance, and it cannot be stated too often. Who you were is not who you are by the washing of regeneration and the word of God.

Don't leave your freedom and ability to move forward in the hands of irrational people. Paul states that you are justified by the experience of being washed by the blood of Christ. Justification states that you are no longer under penalty of God's wrath and judgment, which gives you peace with God as written in Romans 5:1. By the way, who God sets free is indeed free. He sets before you an open door that no one can shut; walk in it with the authority he gives you with boldness. Don't listen to those who constantly want to point you to where you are coming from and who you used to be. Find comfort and solace in Paul's message to the Corinthians in 2 Corinthians 5:17, "Therefore if any man be in Christ, he is a new creature: old things are passed away; behold, all things are become new." Do not spend your precious time distracted by those who do not wish to see you climb and fulfill your purpose.

The Lord told Jeremiah, "Be not afraid of their faces, for I am with thee to deliver thee" (Jeremiah 1:8). There are two types of people you need to be aware of; unfortunately, you will find these two in the church just as they are in the world. One is those who feel like they are holier than others, and if you have a checkered past, you can never meet God's criteria for ministry. They will let you stay in the waiting room until you die or become discouraged. Two, others who have not gotten past their past are determined to hold you where they are. One reason is that if you move on and

114

become successful and prosper, it makes them look worse remaining in their situation. Therefore, whatever they can do to hold you, hostage, they will try it. Sometimes, you must physically separate yourself from others to progress or fulfill your call to ministry. If their rearview mirror about you is more significant than the windshield, shake them off; they are hindrances.

In Luke 7:36cf, Jesus was invited to meat at the house of Simon, a Pharisee. There came this woman known in the city as a sinner. Little is recorded about her history, but her reputation speaks of the person she was. She got in without invitation but with conviction, washed Jesus' feet with her tears, wiped them with her hair, anointed them with the ointment from her broken alabaster box, and constantly kissed his feet.

Simon said within himself, "This man, if he were a prophet, would have known who and what manner of woman this is that touchet him." But Jesus knew his thoughts and told him he had something to say to him. In short, the man with more debts forgiven will show a greater appreciation for forgiveness. Simon couldn't grasp the power of forgiveness that Jesus brought into the world. The narrowness of his mind and his willingness to define this woman based solely on her history prevented him from recognizing what Jesus was able to do.

Another prime example is the woman at Sychar's well, mentioned in John 4. She had five previous husbands and was having a sixth, which wasn't hers. For the same reasons, John tells us that Jesus "must needs go through Samaria" because this woman was there with a checkered past. Jesus did not mention her past to hold her hostage to it. Instead, he mentions it to prove to her that he knows who she is and the character traits of her life. The past story of her life would not be the prologue to her future. Just like he has done for others and will do for anyone in the future, he will not use one's checkered past as a hurdle for one's destiny. That approach is something fundamentally lacking among us today. She, like many today, was (apparently) rejected by those of high moral standards who walked far from her because of character issues that did not align with those of the righteous. We will do good in our community if we align ourselves with God's word and treat people the same way Jesus would. The Samaritan woman was known in her community, not for a reputable reason.

However, that's exactly the person Jesus wanted to talk to because he came not to call the righteous but sinners to repentance, Luke 5:32. His disciples were uncomfortable that he was taking this journey through Samaria. She had a one-on-one encounter with Jesus that forever revolutionized her life. Jesus told her He would give her a well of living water "springing up" into everlasting life. It is a fitting example of why one's dark past is not a deterrent or a detriment to change and a bright future. The immediate expiation of her past gave her a message of gratitude and an invitation to her community.

Ironically, the Bible tells us that she went and told the men, "Come, see a man, which told me all things that ever I did: is not this the Christ?" (John 4:29, KJV). Please don't hold me hostage to my past. My old things have passed away, and behold, and all things have become new (2 Corinthians 5:17).

CHAPTER TEN

RAHAB THE HARLOT

R ahab, the harlot (or prostitute as she was known in Jericho, recorded in Joshua 1), had her house strategically located on top of the outer wall of the double walls built to secure the city of Jericho. Everything about the story of Rahab was strategically, professionally, geographically, and ethnically designed to fulfill God's plan, although it had moral questions attached. What are the chances that Rahab's house and lifestyle were positioned on the wall of Jericho by chance? The foreknowledge of God, his divine providence, or his purpose for her life placed her at the crucial entry point into Jericho. As we take a brief look at her story, it should not be surprising that God does not see through the eyes of men. God has no obligation to follow what man considers standard procedure.

He does not use one's history as a roadblock to hinder him from using him to fulfill his purpose. Rahab was known as one who receives men. That's the person God was looking for because he needed her to give intelligence to the spies as Joshua made strategic plans to take the city of

Jericho. The location of her house was critical, as was the structural layout. Her profession contributed to the protection of the spies. "From the presence of flax upon the room and a stock of scarlet (or crimson) thread in the house, it has been supposed that she was engaged in the manufacture of linen and the art of dyeing" (Merrill F. Unger). God will use the very thing you have, your past experiences, struggles, pains, and the dark sides of your life, to heal others while turning your life around. One should be proud to echo that God wanted me because of these scars and my history. The change he brought into my life is a testament to what he can do with similar or worse lives.

Receiving men, as her custom was, made her a prime candidate for giving the spies access to her home. This was just what God needed to gain intelligence about Jericho and set up an undercover agent in the land. She had a bad reputation, and her character was not welcomed in Jericho. That was the reason it was reported that men had entered her house, triggering the inquiry. It was not long after the men entered her house that something in her heart manifested in a unique way that no one saw coming. In like manner, your scars, bruises, wounds, brokenness, and downfalls are experiences he wants to use to show others what he can do.

It is fascinating that we repeatedly see where God used people's character or profession for his glory and, likewise, to teach us lessons. This time, the men she received in her house were spies sent by Joshua to spy out the land. She received these men, not for the same purpose that she was known, but she received and protected God's two spies for God to accomplish his take over and destruction of Jericho. Rahab was strategically positioned where God wanted her, and her lifestyle fitted the character God wanted to use. It was common for men to enter her house because she was a harlot. God can use anything and anyone to fulfill his purpose.

While God is not the author of evil and never condones it, he often finds a way to bring good even out of evil. In Rabbinic texts, Rahab is described as an innkeeper. Rahab's character makes much sense that the spies would go into her house by God's influence or direction, which appeared normal. It also makes sense that she could be resourceful in providing intelligence to the spies about Jericho's general operations.

The first instinct is to judge and characterize her lifestyle. The second is to question under what circumstance the spies would justify going into a harlot's house. Something to remember as we contemplate this story is what the apostle stated in 1 Corinthians 1:28: "God has chosen what is insignificant and despised in the world-what is viewed as nothing-to bring to nothing what is viewed as something" (CSB)

She hid the men in the ceiling of her house's roof and lied to protect them. One will undoubtedly ask, how is this God's plan if she lied? The truth that God does not work according to man's approval. Before one begins to assess the work of God, one needs to know that the work of God, by the Holy Spirit, cannot be discovered with natural eyes. God's prerogative determines who or what is clean and usable for his glory. That's what Peter did not discern when he presumptuously told the Lord he did not eat common or unclean things.

She exercised faith in God and confidence in his ability to deliver the city of Jericho into the hands of the Israelites, based on the report she had received as they journeyed from Egypt to Canaan. With that in mind, Rahab was convinced that Jericho would also fall into their hands; therefore, she pleaded her cause for sparing her life and the lives of her family based on her excellent deed of protecting them.

Grace and mercy look beyond your past and allow you to make changes. Kindness reciprocates, or at least it should. It is the fundamental reason that many of us get the opportunity to move on with success. The spies agreed to spare her family, but they were advised to gather in one place. In order for them to be protected, the spies must be able to identify her house on the conquest. Therefore, she was told to hang a scarlet thread outside her window. It would be an identifiable mark that the spies would be looking to see.

Placing a scarlet thread on her window symbolized the deliverance of the children of Israel from Egypt when the death angel identified the houses by the blood on the doorposts and the lintels and passed over them.

Likewise, it was a type of the redeeming blood of Christ by which we escape the wrath of God, being washed and redeemed by his sacrifice on the cross.

Suffice it to say that this woman's lifestyle would eliminate her from many conversations today, and she most likely would be deemed as damned and unworthy, but God uses the base things of the earth to confound the wise. Rahab is a prime example. The finish matters more than the start. What became of Rahab after the defeat of Jericho? Here is what Merrill F. Unger writes:

> *At the taking of Jericho the spies, under the command of Joshua, took Rahab and her relatives out of her house, and removed them to a place of safety outside the camp of Israel (Josh. 6:22, 23), and thus made good their oath. The narrator adds, 'And she dwelleth in Israel unto this day,' not necessarily implying that she was still alive at the time he wrote, but that the family of strangers, of which she was reckoned the head, continued to dwell among the children of Israel. As regards Rahab herself, we learn from Matthew 1:5 that she became the wife of Salmon, the son of Naason, and the mother of Boaz, Jessie's grandfather. The suspicion naturally arises that Salmon may have been one of the spies whose life she saved, and that gratitude for so great a benefit led in his case to a more tender passion, and obliterated the memory of any past disgrace attached to her name. But however this may be, it is certain,*

on the authority of Matthew, that Rahab became the mother of the line from which sprung David, and eventually Christ; for that the Rahab mentioned by Matthew is the harlot is as certain as that David in the genealogy is the same person as David in the book of Samuel.

Who would have thought such a story could be part of God's plan? Only when one looks back at the journey and process can his finite mind conclude that it must be God who was working his purpose out. Think about the story of Elimelech found in the book of Ruth. Elimelech moved his family to the land of Moab because the famine was ravishing his country. One can conclude that he made a difficult decision that did not serve his family well, though at first, they had made a great decision. That is how it appeared. History shows that a vast number of people have made great sacrifices. How much must one sacrifice to fulfill God's purpose in his life?

As Naomi returned to her homeland from Moab, she bore the scars of a widow, a childless mother, and the burden of her husband's decision. In the eyes of the ordinary man, the blame was on Elimelech. He decided to move to Moab because of the famine. Looking at the result, one might say it would have been better if they had remained in their homeland. However, the things of God are always foolishness with man. God never follows norms in his plan and purpose for our lives that will bring him glory and fulfill his agenda. Naomi was distraught as she made her journey back home. Naomi had no treasure. She had no family, and her future was dark. However, unknown to man, God was working his purpose behind the scenes.

Repeatedly, history shows that God turned unfortunate situations into incredible, unimaginable stories. The unfortunate deaths of Elimelech, Marlon, and Chilion (as recorded in the book of Ruth) left Nahomi as a widow and childless in Mohab.

It is difficult for people to get past others' past. Every time one is inclined to judge someone else by their scars or hold them hostage to their past, it reminds me of Jesus' approach to the woman taken in adultery and those who accused and brought her. Christ wrote on the ground in his wisdom, care, compassion, and knowledge of the hearts of the woman's accusers. They were willing and ready to stone her under Moses' law but needed to remember or realize they were not in a better position than she was. People find it easy to identify other people's scars, hoping they disguise theirs by doing so. It is always easier to say look over there and not over here because I do not want you to see my scars, so I keep pointing out the other person's scars.

Let's consider ourselves before we start ripping the scabs off others' scars. Everyone has scars, visible or invisible. Moral failures can scar people and others through the emotional pains they experience. One can only imagine what Jesus wrote on the ground based on the reaction of each of the accusers and then telling them bluntly, "He that is without sin among you, let him first cast a stone at her."

Before climbing into a chair of injustice and judging others, it is imperative to listen to the voice of the Apostle Paul, who gives instructions from what he experienced. The Holy Spirit "divinely" inspired him as he wrote in Galatians 6: 1, "Brethren, if a man be overtaken in a fault, ye which are spiritual, restore such a one in the spirit of meekness; considering thyself, lest thou also be tempted."

If everyone follows these instructions, it will heal his emotional scars, and those with unpleasant pasts can move on and build a healthier life and a better world.

Sometimes, our scars are self-inflicted by the choices we make. Still, this is no reason for others to judge us. I made mention of Saul the Hebrew, a Pharisee of the Pharisee whose history could go back to the death of Stephen in Acts 7:58, where participants in and witnesses to Stephen's death laid down their clothes at his feet. That was the beginning of a journey of hate and religious bigotry.

His continued radicalization under Jewish law and customs and his continued ridicule, ill-treatment, and imprisonment of Christians scarred his reputation for generations.

However, despite that, God had his eyes on him to use his zeal, determination, and knowledge for his glory. With that in mind, at the height of his bigotry and cruelty, Christ met him on his way to Damascus, manifested his presence by a shining light, called him by his name, knocked him off his mule, and transformed him with his incredible power.

Undoubtedly, we could draw more examples from the Scriptures of people judged by their scars and held hostage to their past. Yet, despite our disposition toward others, God can change us so that we look at people differently because God has the power to change the scarred one.

CHAPTER ELEVEN

I WAS NOT GOOD ENOUGH

I was not good enough; an expression echoed in the voice of a lady I will call E.M. I have had numerous conversations with her, and the more we communicated, the worse her story got. Some people appear to be made out of steel. If there is one made of steel, I would not hesitate to attribute that to E.M. I consider her battered and bruised but not broken. Her life story began at an early age when her mother migrated to another country, leaving her in Jamaica in the care of a family member. After years of neglect, abuse, and the lack of proper early childhood education, she felt she would need to work harder than average to succeed. Although she grew up in the church, her life was marred with ups and downs. Eventually, E.M. immigrated to join her mother. It was a joyful experience as she thought her life would improve.

Unfortunately, that feeling was short-lived, as she expressed in her own words, "I got married at the age of 20 and had three children. My life began to spiral downward as my husband got involved in the use and abuse of drugs. He was so influenced by it that he became very abusive. One day, while he was under the influence of crack cocaine, he physically abused me, beat and attempted to strangle me. He left me in the house unconscious, but with the help of God, I survived. I decided this was more than I could tolerate, so I took my children and left the country for six months. Upon my return, the government relocated me to a shelter under the Battered Wife Act. For two years, I could not tell anyone where I lived because of the violence I experienced. I filed for divorce, and he was deported because of other violations of the law he had committed."

Although E.M. grew up in the church, she had not committed her life to Christ and Christianity. Two years later, she got into another relationship that produced another child out of wedlock. During this time, she visited a church; the word and conviction took hold of her heart, and she decided to follow the Lord. The pastor pushed her to get married as a matter of principle. They decided to marry each other in her attempt to follow biblical guidelines. The marriage produced another child. Her husband also decided to follow the Lord two years after the marriage. However, he was not faithful in the marriage, often cheating on her. His unfaithfulness continued while he was in the church. As a result of that, he became verbally abusive and eventually divorced her. The wounds of her heart and emotions got more profound as she became a mother of five children struggling to stay afloat.

Despite the heartaches, grief, pain, and disappointment, she held on to her faith in the Lord as she hoped for a better day. Better days were not soon coming. E.M. was a competent driver, and she was assigned to drive the Sunday school bus. In doing so, she developed a good relationship with the youths and unofficially worked with them. "There was a vacancy for someone to work with the young people. I applied for the position, was given two interviews, and was rejected, though I was trained. I was nominated for the position of Sunday School Director, but it was offered to another young lady who was not trained for the position, and she refused to take it. As a result, it remained vacant for a while." I often wonder why we preach and teach about the redemptive blood of Christ if we do not believe in its efficacy. Why do we tell others that the blood of Jesus can wash and make them clean no matter what they have done if we do not honestly believe it or accept the finished work of grace?

How do we justify teaching 2 Corinthians 5:14 if we do not believe it is true? "Therefore, if any man be in Christ, he is a new creature: old things are passed away; and behold, all things are become new." If that is true, why do we continue to reject what Christ accepts? Are we in the mindset of Peter, who dared to confront Jesus about what was common or unclean? Although Isaiah's prophesies were geared toward Judah, he fundamentally prophesied about the coming Messiah, whose plan was to forgive sins and give new life. The prophet made it clear in the first chapter. "Come now, and let us reason together, saith the Lord:

though your sins be as scarlet, they shall be as white as snow; though they are red like crimson, they shall be as wool" (Isaiah 1:18). For those who want to tie this to the Old Testament must not forget that when Jesus was asked to read the text at the beginning of his earthly ministry, he declaratively read from Isaiah as is mentioned in Luke 4:18, quoting from Isaiah 61.

> *"The Spirit of the Lord God is upon me, because he hath anointed me to preach the gospel to the poor; he hath sent me to heal the broken hearted, to preach deliverance to the captives, and recovering of sight to the blind, to set at liberty them that are bruised. To preach the acceptable year of the Lord. And he closed the book, and he gave it again to the minister, and sat down. And the eyes of all them that were in the synagogue were fastened on him. And he began to say unto them, this day is this Scripture fulfilled in your ears" (Luke 4:18-21).*

Jesus did not come to call the righteous. He did not come to minister to those who were well. He came to call sinners unto repentance and reconcile the world to himself. Jesus heals broken hearts and puts shattered pieces back together in the reconciliation process. He sets at liberty those who are bruised. The primary verb Luke used to describe bruised means to crush, break in pieces, shatter, and smite through. Why are so many preachers, pastors, and church people not part of the healing process? Why do we keep aggravating people whom Jesus has set free? What is the justification for pointing people to where they are coming from instead of helping them reach their destiny? You would think we are all aware that the blood of Jesus is powerful enough to cleanse one from his past. It breaks my heart to see the abuse generated even from the platform and behind the pulpit by those who disguise themselves behind the Bible and fabricate the manifestation or revelation of the Spirit. E.M. blamed herself for making the mistake of sharing her testimony, which she believed was used against her. "When I got saved, in my ignorance, I shared my testimony with the church and some of what I was dealing with at the time, and I believe it was used against me."

It becomes harder to deal with when the ones who should be helping you to heal are the ones who are making your pain worse. "One of the elders did not want her daughter around me, and some did not want me around the young people because they believed I was not a good influence for the youths because of my past life, which they did not know about except for what I had told them. However, the more they tried to keep the young people away from me, the more God saw it fit to use me in their lives. I thank God for the few he had placed in my life who stood with me and became a voice for me when my voice was stolen by those who tried to oppress me while the call of God was on my life." She continued talking about her experience with a designated preacher who made her a targeted subject. "There were times I was made to feel like an outcast because of my past. I remember one Sunday, a sister preached and said, 'There is nothing my husband could ever do to make me divorce him,' as I think of it, what came to my mind was that I did not divorce my husband; he divorced me. At that time, two of us were going through the experience. The other couple had left the ministry, and I remained the only one there. I can recall others looking at me while she was making those statements. I don't know whether it was her conscience or what, but at the end of the service, she came to me and apologized and said, the message was not directed to me." I can only imagine being blatantly targeted and victimized in a church that should be a city of refuge.

Before that, E.M. had experienced one of the darkest moments in her life during the cheating and verbal abuse of her second husband; combined with the other experiences, it began to take its toll on E.M.'s emotions, and she felt it was too much to bear, but for the grace and help of God, she would not be here to share her story. She was pushed to the brink of suicidal ideation with the opportunity to do it. This is how she remembers that moment.

One day, while driving this huge seventy-two-seater school bus, broken and in tears from my second husband's cheating and verbal abuses, he cursed me out and tried to destroy my life. While driving along the road, the bus was empty; I was in tears. I heard a voice say, Just put the bus over the bridge. I was about to do it when I felt a hand on my shoulder, and a voice said that suicide will separate you from the Lord. At that time, I remember the Scripture said nothing can separate you from the love of God; I get that Scripture. But I kept hearing the same voice saying go over the bridge, just go over. It was then I felt a hand squeeze my shoulder and said suicide will separate you from the love of God. I wasn't versed in the Scripture, but that's what I heard. I was driving the bus up the road toward the bridge, where there was a deep precipice. I was driving on this road where the area was not built up, and things appeared blurry, but I kept driving and coming up to the edge.

It was then I heard another voice, and I did not know it was the Spirit of God, but I felt someone standing close to me with his hand holding on tight to my shoulder, and the voice said to me, The road will not adjust to suit you, you must adjust to suit the road. And I heard the same thing repeated. I kept driving on the road's edge, but the bus kept going as if I didn't have control. Although I had been doing this for years, the bus just kept going like it was gliding on the corner, but it kept going from corner to corner until I made it past where I could put it over the bridge. Somehow, God pulled me through and passed this tragic moment. Years later, as I faced more obstacles in my life, God kept me.

I remember ministering at a convention when those words came back to me. The road will not adjust to suit you; you must adjust to suit the road. Then, I was able to apply them to say life will not adjust to suit you; you must adjust to suit life. At that time, some of the people who used to fight against me at my church were at that convention where I was preaching that Saturday night. The Spirit of God took me (I am not flexible), and I saw when my body contoured to the left and the right and went down. It was like balls were being thrown at me, and I had to adjust. And as I adjusted, the balls would pass me, and it kept happening.

Nevertheless, God pulled the church through that night with a mighty move. It was after that service I realized what God was saying to me. Things are going to come in your life. You do not have to stand there and be knocked over; adjust your thinking, adjust yourself to suit the hiccups in life. The hiccups in life don't have to decide your future. They do not come to destroy you; they come to make you stronger, that was the word. Ever since that time, I learned how to adjust to circumstances that present themselves in my life.

As riveting as this portion of E.M.'s story sounds, it is only a synopsis of her journey. It seems like some people's lives are designed to be examples of resilience, strength, and overcoming obstacles to help others realize that despite what they are going through, hold on to God's unchanging hand, and he will pull you through the dark valleys. Her life fits my theory that some scars are for God's glory. No one wants to experience what she has been through and continues to go through. Today, despite how God has used her to touch many lives, she is still being judged by her scars and is held hostage to her past. Recently, she has done all the preparatory work, passed all the exams, and met all the criteria to be licensed as a minister in her organization. Still, her history shows that she was divorced and remarried decades ago. Because of that, she was not shown the courtesy of a one-on-one conversation about the issue. She is still held hostage to her past. It makes me wonder who has the upper hand. If God can use you to change lives for his glory and the benefit of his children, what if some men chose not to give you a certificate? Unfortunately, some men and women feel they are Lord over God's heritage or have the final word on who progresses or redresses in God's kingdom. Let heaven record your work, and may that work speak for you. Man can always find fault with you if God says well done. In the end, it is God who rewards the work you have done. When he says, "Well done," he will not require the approval of any church leader to do so.

CHAPTER TWELVE

THE CULTURE OF IGNORANCE

A culture of ignorance has permeated the church over decades if not centuries. As a result, many lives have been negatively impacted. Unfortunately, many who have an influential voice in the church do not have the wisdom to guide them in using it. A combination of ignorance and arrogance is to be avoided because they can cause peril in the lives of others. For many decades, if not centuries, hundreds of thousands have suffered because of the ignorance and arrogance of others. Understandably, but no less effectively, many have become victims of the sincere ignorance of influencers. In speaking of sincere ignorance, I mean those with good intent but lack the knowledge of and understanding of the Bible and use their opinion or another's interpretation to determine how they should treat another person. On the other hand, some are willingly ignorant. The willingly ignorant defy biblical interpretation to maintain control and dictate how you should live your life.

I grew up in a culture of ignorance and arrogance. During testimony service, leaders would draw close to a brother, sister, or young minister, whisper in his ear, and say, "Don't testify tonight; you are going to preach." Often, preachers got up to preach, read a portion of Scripture, and said nothing about the text. They would go off on a tangent or down some rabbit holes and attribute it to the revelation of the Holy Spirit. One of the famous statements was, open your mouth, and the Lord will fill it with words. Preachers often take Bible verses or portions of texts at face value without understanding the context or application, torture it, and fit it wherever they feel necessary to boost their ego or target the vulnerable. The apostle Paul, in his instructions to Timothy, told him, "Study to show thyself approved unto God, a workman that needeth not to be ashamed, rightly dividing the word of truth" (2 Timothy 2:1). He also told him to 'shun profane and vain babblings: for they will increase unto more ungodliness" (2 Timothy 2:16).

Nothing but an open Bible was accepted whether or not it had the proper interpretation. It took a long time for the church's elders to accept a preacher getting into the pulpit to preach with notes. It was considered preaching in self and not depending on the Holy Spirit. They considered writing a sermon lacking the Spirit's divine leading and, therefore, could not come from the Lord. Gradually, the church introduced leadership training and emphasized the value of homiletics and hermeneutics. Eventually, they realized that anointed preaching was not something filled with emotional flare-ups and babblings, but the understanding of and delivery of biblical interpretation shaped the believers' lives.

Many came to the church with scars and were made to live with wounds. Nothing is worse than using the Bible to hurt and not to heal. The COVID-19 pandemic has taken multiple millions of lives and had its most devastating impact because everyone was ignorant of what it was and what approach was needed to mitigate its effect. Hosea gives an insight into the danger of ignorance. "My people are destroyed for lack of knowledge" (Hosea 4:6). Not only are the ignorant in danger, but those on the receiving end of one's ignorance are in equal danger, if not more. Some of us grew up in the church when there were so-called watchdogs overlooking everyone. One must admit that sound principles and ethical guidelines were needed to help shape the lives of young and new believers. At the same time, many lives were torn apart out of ignorance and arrogance. The virtue of patience was virtually nonexistent. The tolerance level was zero. A Christ-like attitude was rarely sought after.

To this day, some people in the church believe that the only tool necessary is a hammer. It allows them to hit everything on the head, not realizing that if some things are hit on the head, it might cause irreparable damage. The principle approach given to the Galatians by Paul was either not known or deliberately ignored. "Brethren, if a man be overtaken in a fault, ye which are spiritual, restore such an one in the spirit of meekness; considering thyself, lest thou also be tempted" (Galatians 6:1). One who is spiritual is considered as being filled with, and governed by the Holy Spirit which also means, that one has a firm understanding and application of God's word. That was relevant then as it is now. While the average person tries to walk right and live in sanctification, it is clear that no one is immune to making mistakes. Therefore, while the inclination is there to judge others, one should always be aware of their equal vulnerabilities. "Wherefore let him that thinketh he standeth take heed lest he fall" (1 Corinthians 10:12). It should encourage everyone to make an internal evaluation of oneself while assessing others.

Some people are made to live not only with the memories of their past but also with the pain. Nothing is more paralyzing and debilitating than being forced to carry baggage you want to let go of but are constantly reminded of. Because of that, many have been unable to establish and maintain meaningful relationships.

In his wisdom, Solomon tells us, "Death and life are in the power of the tongue: and they that love it shall eat the fruit thereof" (Proverbs 18:21). We learn from that statement that what a man says can determine his future and fortune. Likewise, what he says could cause his death and also the death of others. Solomon wants us to know that our words will profoundly impact us and also affect those who hear us. People sometimes think what they say affects only those about whom it is said. Contrary to that concept or perception, what emerges from our mouths reflects our nature and character. What comes out of one's mouth is not random or detached from the person who speaks. Jesus speaks of the power and effect of words and their origination. He clarified that speaking words of blasphemy against the Holy Ghost shall not be forgiven because it takes time to develop within one's heart before those words come out of one's mouth. Because of that, the words one speaks could be to his peril and the peril of others. The scenario he was painting is that the tree bears fruit from its nature, and you can determine the tree by the fruit. So those among the multitude who chose to speak evil against the Father, Son, and Holy Ghost put themselves in imminent danger because what comes out of the mouth is an overflow of what's in the heart. Here is what he says in Matthew 12:34-37:

> *O generation of vipers, how can ye, being evil, speak good things? For out of the abundance of the heart, the mouth speaketh. A good man out of the good treasure of the heart bringeth forth good things: and an evil man out of the evil treasure bringeth forth evil things. But I say unto you, That every idle word that men shall speak, they shall give account thereof in the day of judgment. For by the words thou shalt be justified, and by thy words thou shalt be condemned.*

The reference to 'abundance' speaks of a superabundance or a surplus, from where we find an overflow. Implying that whatever comes from the mouth is an overflow of what the heart stockpiles. The 'treasure the heart' speaks of a deposit of wealth. That suggests that wealth, in other words, is whatever one invests in, is what the heart stores, good or evil. In essence, Solomon and Jesus want us to know that our words will undoubtedly have a negative or positive outcome. Therefore, be aware that there is death and life in the power of the tongue, so proceed with caution and evaluate the outcome. Sometimes, our approach to life is too casual, and how we speak to and about others is too nonchalant or carefree. Our words should be with grace, seasoned with salt (metaphorically) to heal wounds and not inflict pain. Recognizing how powerful words are, everyone should be cautious before speaking to or about someone concerning something one likes or dislikes. One's motive should always be to help. Wisdom, knowledge, and understanding are three indispensable tools everyone should have in their toolbox. Imagine if everyone is wise enough to know what approach to take when trying to help someone. Jesus tells us in Matthew 10:16 to be "wise as serpents, and harmless as doves." I like the Amplified Bible's version of Proverbs 4:5-10.

Get [skillful and godly] wisdom! Acquire understanding [actively seek spiritual discernment, mature comprehension, and logical interpretation]! Do not forget nor turn away from the words of my mouth. ⁶ Do not turn away from her (Wisdom) and she will guard and protect you; Love her, and she will watch over you.

⁷ The beginning of wisdom is: Get [skillful and godly] wisdom [it is preeminent]! And with all your acquiring, get understanding [actively seek spiritual discernment, mature comprehension, and logical interpretation]. [8] Prize wisdom [and exalt her], and she will exalt you; She will honor you if you embrace her. [9] She will place on your head a garland of grace; She will present you with a crown of beauty and glory. [10] Hear, my son, and accept my sayings, And the years of your life will be many.

How about being knowledgeable that people are not of the same temperament and, therefore, cannot be approached in the same way? That would make a difference in making the first step toward rebuking, correcting, and instructing others. And then, one of the most important of the three is understanding. Understanding is the framework that holds it all together. That's why we are instructed to get understanding in all our getting. It teaches us the method of application. It helps us realize that no one-size-fits-all solution to dealing with humans exists. Although one thing just worked for John, it may not work for Jane. The culture of ignorance that has disrupted and to a greater extent, destroyed many lives cannot be ignored if there is going to be a positive impact on the lives of others.

CHAPTER THIRTEEN

PREPARING THE SKEPTIC

God told Ananias that Saul was coming to see him in Damascus, and his reply was, "Lord, I have heard by many of this man, how much evil he hath done to thy saints at Jerusalem: And here he hath authority from the priests to bind all that call on thy name" (Acts 9:13-14).

But the Lord said unto him, "Go thy way: for he is a chosen vessel unto me, to bear my name before the Gentiles, and kings, and the children of Israel" (Acts 9:15). Right after he received his sight, baptized, and gained strength he started to preach the very Christ he had recently encountered.

From that day, he relentlessly preached and declared his newfound faith. He was so zealous and impacted his community so profoundly that he became a target of his opposition, and those considered him a hypocrite or a betrayer.

It was evident that he had had a changed life as he continued to preach and teach about Christ, yet it took fourteen years for skeptics in the church to give him the right hand of fellowship (Galatians 2:9).

Fourteen years of incredible service to the Lord, fourteen years of scrutiny, and fourteen years of holding him hostage to his past. Thousands of people find themselves in similar situations where others refuse to release them from their history. Because of that, their lives have been unproductive, and their spiritual lives have become dormant.

If you look around today, you will see a self-righteous approach to how individuals are ill-treated because of what is known of their past. Change is real, especially regarding the efficaciousness of Christ's redemptive blood and his willingness to cast one's sins in the sea of forgetfulness.

The callousness and unempathetic attitude demonstrated by those who fail to adopt the "golden rule" principle of "do unto others as you would have others do unto you" drives these kinds of selfish behavior.

I have seen people unwilling to pull others past their past, who eventually fall into worse situations, and hope not to be a hostage to their history when they have moved on or made corrections.

Do not judge me by my scars. You do not know how I got them; you have no clue about my journey to be where I am. You have no idea what I've been through to get where I am. Please do not hold me hostage to my past. God has forgiven me, changed my life, and made something out of nothing.

A person may have a tumultuous past and lived a messy life, but by the blood of Jesus, our eternal sacrifice, he has been cleansed and given a new lease on life. This experience is not temporary but is perpetual by God's gift of love and grace, who is willing to expiate the stains of sin and set the captive free.

The apostle Paul's words to the Romans, "There is therefore now no condemnation to them which are in Christ Jesus, who walk not after the flesh, but after the spirit" (Romans 8:1), comfort us. One can also find comfort in 1 Corinthians 6:11, "And such were some of you: but you are washed, but you are sanctified, but you are justified in the name of the Lord Jesus, and by the Spirit of our God."

Living in a particular environment, culture, community, family setting, and dynamics can contribute to one becoming physically scarred, not because of what they have done, but because of their surroundings. On the spiritual side of life, no one is exempt from the devil's onslaught. It is why God preemptively provided Christ's advocacy for the bruised and wounded to find healing and hope. If you have not been impacted negatively in life, rejoice; you are the exception.

Being free from being negatively impacted in life is unnatural for most others. Most can identify with Paul's counsel or warning to the Corinthians: reminding them that fornicators, adulterers, idolaters, thieves, drunkards, extortioners, and others considered unrighteous shall not inherit the kingdom of God. The good news is that God knew man's weaknesses and provided restoration through his sacrifice on the cross. Here is the critical thought, "And such were some of you: but you are washed, but you are sanctified, but you are justified in the name of the Lord Jesus, and by the Spirit of our God" (1 Corinthians 6:11).

CHAPTER FOURTEEN

NOT UNIQUE TO STRANGERS

Holding one hostage to his past is not unique to strangers, but it happens in families likewise. Neither is it confined to this generation; the same is true for all ages. Take a look at what happened in Luke 15 with two brothers. Their wealthy father had made provisions for them that they would have enough to start their lives when they grew up. The story does not say whether both sons were hard-working or not. However, the parable shows the younger brother (identified as the Prodigal Son) growing increasingly anxious and desirous of experimenting with life independently. Unwisely and probably lacking maturity, the younger brother demanded that his father give him his portion of the inheritance, and he left home to be on his own. That had to be a shocker to his entire family. However, they did not hinder him from going and proved that he could not navigate life without guidance and maturity.

As his father's wisdom predicted, though we do not have a verbal or written report of his feelings, his action tells us what he was thinking. He "wasted his substance with riotous living." His father was heartbroken and surprised by his son's abrupt and impulsive request, but if the lesson had to do with one's free will, the father had no choice but to allow him to learn from his mistakes. After evaluating irrational actions, lessons learned from one's assessment are more poignant and will yield longer-lasting fruit. One of the many lessons depicted in this story is the father's wisdom, compassion, and care. It also shows how God our heavenly Father will show love and compassion to everyone who recognizes his mistakes and makes amends. Through repentance and return, he will find the Father's hands open to welcome him home.

The young man went on a spending spree, and it wasn't long before he exhausted his resources and became desperate. The example leads one to believe the young man had drifted into abandoned and rejected places. Luke reports that after gathering his portion of wealth, he journeyed into a faraway country, not wanting to be discovered by family and friends. The risks and rewards did not match up. "And when he had spent all, there arose a mighty famine in that land; and he began to be in want" (Luke 15:14). Yes, this is a parable illustrated by Jesus, but a parable illustrates a moral attitude or a religious principle. It leads me to believe that the parable has religious connotations and is an essential lesson for all.

FEEDING SWINE

Out of want and desperation, the Prodigal Son (Luke 15:11-32) degraded his prestige (based on Jewish culture and religious practices) as a Jewish boy. He joined himself with a citizen of that far country where he went to live, and his assignment was to feed swine in the field. The young man first violated his religious beliefs and practices by accepting the job assignment to feed swine. Second, from degradation and starvation to desperation, he fed himself from the remains of swine leftovers without being authorized. When one considers this as a real-life story, it happens over a period of time. So, one would have time to reflect and evaluate the gradual decline of his situation. In any culture, feeding swine as the only available job is not prestigious.

The Prodigal Son had fallen to the lowest level of degradation where he was eating the remains of swine food, and as Jesus stated, "and no man gave unto him." Finding oneself in that position is not where one aspires to be. If one considers where he was in terms of wealth not long ago, it shows the internal struggle he had to deal with. How worse could it get for him? The answer one will never know. However, judging how far he had fallen and how quickly, the chances were high that it could have gotten worse. It was at that moment of consciousness, brokenness, introspection, and reflection that he concluded that despite his past mistakes and lack of good judgment, despite returning empty-handed, emaciated, embarrassed, and broken, he would be better off being at home without the status of a son than being in a strange land feeding swine and eating their food. Pride and shame, and considering what others will think and say, hinder many from going or coming back home. One lesson from this story is that it doesn't matter how far you have fallen or by what circumstance it happens; whether by adverse situations or deliberate acts, the journey home will always be clear. Being restored is fundamentally the top priority.

Nevertheless, this will not happen until one makes a hard decision after reaching a serious conclusion. After coming to himself: here is what the young man said, "How many hired servants of my father's have bread enough to spare, and I perish with hunger! I will arise and go to my father, and will say unto him, Father, I have sinned against heaven, and before thee, And I am no more worthy to be called thy son: make me one of thy hired servants" (Luke 15:17-19).

CHAPTER FIFTEEN

GOING BACK HOME

He decided to go back home in repentance. It must have been one of the most challenging moves he had to make, but the best move in the long run. Whenever one returns to the Father, it is always a welcomed gesture. In the Old Testament, God promised to marry the returning backslider before grace was abundant. "' Return, O backsliding children,' says the LORD; 'for I am married to you. I will take you, one from a city and two from a family, and I will bring you to Zion. And I will give you shepherds according to My heart, who will feed you with knowledge and understanding" (Jeremiah 3:14 NKJV). From a distance, God is watching us and has provided everything needed for a welcome home. His father saw him and did not express anger or disappointment; he welcomed him out of his heart of love, care, and compassion. The same is not true for everyone. He was vilified by his older brother, who was only concerned about his brother's reckless past and his return to rob him of what he considered his portion. Unfortunately, one will (not everyone) have a similar experience returning to a church to be reconciled with God.

There was no heart of compassion and care. He found all the reasons his brother did not deserve the treatment his father requested. If God dealt with us the way our attitude deserves, we would not be where we are today. However, we rejoice in knowing that he looks beyond our faults and sees our needs.

His brother expressed no appreciation for the life of his wayward sibling. He showed no concern for him. He was heartless, uncompassionate, selfish, and greedy. One can only imagine his thoughts concerning his brother for him to show no compassion on his return. The only thing on his mind was the material loss he projected. His older brother had no insight into their father's thinking and plans. Based on the father's action, it appears he was anticipating the return of his younger son, and therefore, he was putting things in place for his reunion unknown to his brother. No matter how many have returned to the Lord, there is room for more. Similarly, like our heavenly Father, his earthly father was willing to look past his past and help him in the restoration process.

I can only imagine what it was like when he told the history of his story to those who had the interest and compassion to listen. The heart and kindheartedness of the father are a testament to how Christ wants us to love and care for each other. How many of us will support needy brothers and sisters even if they have caused their demise? Who is willing to put himself in his position? Who will follow Paul's instructions to the Galatians in chapter 6:1?

"Brethren, if a man be overtaken in a fault, ye which are spiritual, restore such an one in the spirit of meekness; considering thyself, lest thou also be tempted." Too many of us have rejected that instruction or are ignorant of it. People are not willing to look beyond one's mistakes but are bent on holding them hostage to their past. We must remember that none of us are perfect; all have sinned and come short of the glory of God (Romans 3:23). The examples Christ gives us reject everything about our unwillingness to look beyond one's mistakes. If holding one hostage to their past was part of God's plan, he would not have a dependable servant today to carry the message of hope and reconciliation. The only one that God held hostage to his past is Lucifer, who became Satan.

All through history, God's servants have had flaws or checkered pasts. Some feel they should keep an edge over others because their deeds, failures, or weaknesses are not publicly known. That is the reason why those men who brought the woman to Jesus and told him they caught her in the act of adultery, and therefore, in following Moses' law, she should be stoned to death. But God, who knows even the hidden things of the heart, would not fall for their pretense of innocence. Today, many people want to make your failures and mistakes the central theme of their conversations to hide and conceal their shortcomings. Here is something in the story of the Prodigal Son's parable that might be overlooked that I want to bring to your attention. The whole process of repentance and reconciliation happened between the father and son outside the presence of all others. Wrap your mind around the entire picture that Jesus painted with this parable. The last thing known about this lad was that he was feeding swine and being so deep into starvation that his only alternative was to eat the swine's leftovers for survival. Yet from there, he went home. And his father saw him in the distance, a great way off, and recognized him. Not only did he recognize him, but he ran to meet him out of his heart of compassion. His father did not simply go to meet him to find out what had happened, but he fell on his neck and kissed him. How did he look, and what odor was he carrying? None of those things mattered to the father and perhaps the reason why this level of detail is not recorded in scripture.

The most important thing was seeing his wayward son returning home. As you reflect on the parable, I want to pinpoint a few other things and make it an imaginable literal story. Despite the father's warm welcome, the son's inner conviction of a clear conscience warranted his confession and repentance. Please note that no probational period or ultimatum was given to him, nor what process it would require before he could be assimilated into the family. If you have been in a similar situation, this is how God deals with a backslider or one who has gone astray and returned home. It doesn't matter how battered, bruised, broken, abused, despised, rejected, criticized, or scorned; God will not delay reconciling you to himself. That is instantaneous sanctification—the washing of regeneration by the word. It was only the father and his son in the initial meeting.

Interestingly, his father did not wait for the older brother to come from the field before the celebration started. God is not obligated to give anyone a heads-up or seek one's approval in your restoration process. The servants had no say but to follow their master's instructions. "But the father said to his servants, Bring forth the best robe, and put it on him; and put a ring on his hand, and shoes on his feet: and bring hither the fatted calf, and kill it; and let us eat and be merry: For this my son was dead, and is alive again; he was lost, and is found. And they began to be merry" (Luke 15:22-24). It was a time of reconciliation and rejoicing. The massive celebration was not necessary or contributed to the son's repentance; however, it erased any lingering doubt concerning how much the father loved him and how welcomed he was in coming back home. In the previous parable earlier in the chapter about the rejoicing in finding a lost coin, Jesus states, "Likewise, I say unto you, there is joy in the presence of the angels of God over one sinner that repenteth" (V.10). Not everyone will be happy for you when God restores you. It was evident with the older brother. The one you believe would be most joyful was the most angry. On his way home from the field, he heard the music and celebration and was confused. As he got closer, he asked a servant what was happening; lo and behold, it was his wayward brother who came back home, and shockingly, the father did not turn him away but was having a gigantic celebration. He was angry when he heard the story and refused to enter the celebration. The Father had to go outside and implore him to come in; even then, all he had were complaints, reflections, and rejection. He was utterly void of compassion and the capacity to extend a hand. The elder brother was so angry and withdrawn that his bitter heart refused to recognize him as his brother. "And he answering said to his father, Lo, these many years do I serve thee, neither transgressed I at any time thy commandment; and yet thou never gavest me a kid, that I might make merry with my friends: But as soon as this thy son was come, which have devoured thy living with harlots, thou hast killed for him the fatted calf" (Vs. 29-30). Your redemption and reconciliation are not contingent on the approval of others.

The righteous need not be angry and complain when the sinner is redeemed or the backslider returns. There is nothing to be selfish or jealous about. Be gracious to God for his sustaining grace and be thankful you have remained under his protection and provision. The scribes and Pharisees murmured and complained when Jesus called Levi the publican who followed him, and after that made him a meal, they sat and ate with other publicans and others. They questioned why Jesus ate and drank with publicans and sinners. "And Jesus answering and said unto them, They that are whole need not a physician; but they that are sick. I came not to call the righteous, but sinners to repentance" (Luke 5:31-32). The father's response to a disgruntled son is similar to what Jesus told the Pharisees. "And he said unto him, Son, thou art ever with me, and all that I have is thine. It was meet that we should make merry, and be glad: for this thy brother was dead, and is alive again; and was lost, and is found" (Luke 15:31-32). Maybe he would be happy if the younger brother was never heard from again. His mind was so steeped in the remains of his father's wealth that it blocked his discernment and appreciation for life.

Maybe he would have felt better if he had come home and been told that his brother had returned after taking his portion of wealth and was driven away by his father. Or if he saw him sitting somewhere rejected and dejected so he could lash at him with his tongue and tell him what a waste and letdown to the family he was.

Be aware of those similar to this unforgiving brother who refused to recognize his brother as worthy of redemption. When God favors you, washes you, blesses you, and puts your feet on the rock to stand, look out for those who want to push you back into the mire. All some people want to do is dwell on yesterday's sorrow, not rejoice in the joy of your tomorrow. Holding you hostage to your past and picking at your scars are where some find pleasure. Jesus' declaration about his purpose and ministry on earth, as he read from the prophet Isaiah in Luke 4:18-19 contradicts that approach. Here is what he affirms from Isaiah 61:1-2 "The Spirit of the Lord God is upon me, because he hath anointed me to preach the gospel to the poor, he hath sent me to heal the brokenhearted, to preach deliverance to the captives, and recovering of sight to the blind, to set at liberty them that are bruised. To preach the acceptable year of the Lord." Following Jesus's example, we are called to heal wounds, not cause them.

One old Indian Proverb states, "There is nothing noble in being superior to some other man. True nobility is in being superior to your previous self." We must all grapple with that question as we consider our vulnerabilities. The Prodigal Son falls in the category of backsliders. Unfortunately, hundreds of thousands of people fit this category. The possibility of slipping, sliding, and falling is endless. I introduce the apostle Peter as a prime example. Let me point out a couple of facts. One, Peter was among the first of Jesus' disciples. Jesus saw something special in him and gave him a name to signify what he saw in him. His brother Andrew brought him to Jesus, and immediately, Jesus gave him a name change. "And he brought him to Jesus. And when Jesus beheld him, he said, Thou art Simon the son of Jona: thou shalt be called Cephas, which is by interpretation, a stone" (John 1:42)

Two, the name change to a stone did not immune him. Luke records in Chapter 22 three instances where Peter denied he knew Christ. Not only did he deny that he knew Jesus, but he was also hanging out with the wrong crowd. Previously, in the same chapter, Jesus instructed Peter about Satan's desire to shake him down. "And the Lord said, Simon, Simon, behold, Satan hath desired to have you, that he may sift you as wheat: but I have prayed for thee, that thy faith fail not: and when thou art converted, go strengthen thy brethren" (Luke 22:31-32). One wonders why he was such a target. The fact that Jesus called him "a stone" proves that there was something special about him. The future of his ministry would have a profound impact on the world until this day. The devil wanted to blythe what he sensed in him. Peter's desire to return to his old fishing lifestyle was a sign of backsliding.

Jesus, who named him a stone and told him of the ploy of Satan to destroy him, knew the importance of the ministry that went dormant in him. However, the time was coming for that ministry to come to life, quickened by the power of the Holy Spirit. As a result, Jesus returned to find him at sea and restored him to the Rock ministry he previously identified in him. The ministry of Peter produced more miracles than any other apostle. That's what the devil was trying to prevent. Remember this. Peter preached at Pentecost after the outpouring of the Holy Spirit's baptism, and 3,000 souls received salvation and became church members. That's 3,000 people who escaped the wages of sin, and that's one of the things Satan wanted to avoid.

Not only did he preach one of the most result-orientated salvation sermons ever, but he also manifested the power of God to the beggar at the temple's gate (Acts 3:1-8). More miracles are in Acts 5 about Ananias and his wife, Sapphira, who lied to Peter and died as a consequence. That was another mighty move of God in the life of Peter that drew many more people to the Lord. Because of that, the community's people believed that if they brought their sick loved ones by the wayside, the shadow of Peter would heal them, and their faith never failed. Finally, they called him when Tabitha died, and he raised her back to life by the power of God.

When one looks closely at Peter's life, it has been with many ups and downs. Why do I mention these things about Peter? As much as Peter denied Christ at the most vulnerable time on earth, Christ did not condemn him. He did not hold him hostage to his past. To say that Peter had a checkered past is an understatement. However, when Jesus sat with him, he didn't mention his past; instead, he asked him if he loved him. Jesus wanted to know the condition of his heart, not for his knowledge but for our learning. Let me say without reservation that thousands of Christians worldwide have been in a similar position as Peter. Many became backsliders, falling victim to the devil, while others stumbled and fell. How many have been judged by their past or held hostage to their past and, therefore, have not been able to fulfill the call of God on their lives?

As you read this book, you may see yourself in it. You may see yourself as a victim unable to bring forth what God placed in your heart because others believe they should determine your future, whether you meet God's criteria or fit their model. No one knows at what point in your life God has forgiven you of your past and restored you to fulfill his purpose for your life. At the same time, some contemplate whether anything good can come out of others because of where they come from or the path they take to get where they are. Nothing is new under the sun. Christ was rejected by his nation because of where he was born and the way he grew up. At the outset of Jesus' ministry, when Philip told Nathaniel that he had found Jesus of Nazareth, whom Moses mentioned in the law, he was skeptical about Nazareth's reputation. He pondered if any good thing could come from there. Here is what John records about the encounter.

> *"Philip findeth Nathaniel, and saith unto him, We have found him, of whom Moses in the law, and the prophets, did write, Jesus of Nazareth, the son of Joseph. And Nathaniel said unto him, Can any good thing come out of Nazareth? Philip saith unto him, Come and see. Jesus saw Nathaniel coming to him, and saith of him, Behold an Israelite indeed, in whom is no guile. Nathaniel saith unto him, Whence knowest thou me? Jesus answered and said unto him, Before that Philip called thee, when thou wast under the fig tree, I saw thee. Nathaniel answered and saith unto him, Rabbi, thou art the Son of God; thou art the king of Israel" (John 1:45-49).*

I mention this because Nathaniel was skeptical of Nazareth's reputation, yet he was curious enough to follow Philip when he told him to come and see. Maybe he went so that he would prove his point. But to his surprise, his experience was far beyond his imagination, which led him to discover that something good could come out of Nazareth. Not only did he make the discovery, but Nathaniel had a divine revelation of who Jesus was, hence his declaration that he was the Son of God and king of Israel. Philip did not doubt his testimony, and Jesus did not need Nathaniel's revelation to affirm who he was. However, to clear the skeptic's mind, Jesus spoke directly to him to eliminate his doubts. When God forgives you, cleanses, and restores you, he does not need others to verify, solidify, or qualify his work of grace and restoration.

There will always be a Thomas among the disciples who was fierce enough to tell his fellow laborers that he would not believe unless he saw Jesus, put his finger in the wound in his hand, and thrust his hand in his side. Look around you, and you will (without a doubt) find people with the same mentality as Thomas. They are reluctant to accept the potency of the transforming power of redemption, though they testify of it. Their action suggests that such benefit applies only to those they give the okay as if God has to hear from them. Paul told his young and upcoming minister, Timothy, "Let no man despise thy youth; but be thou an example of the believers, in word, in conversation, in charity, in spirit, in faith, in purity" (1 Timothy 4:12). That is how some people will stop the mouth of the gainsayers. Prove what God has done by the life you live. I have known many people and have spoken to many more whom others rejected, only to watch them rise and outshine all expectations.

CONCLUSION

Your life might not be at the point of gratitude right now because you cannot discern why things are happening. Maybe you have carved out in your mind what the perfect will of God will be like, and it is not going according to plan. Your life might not be as complicated as that of Jacob. But, remember, nothing in Jacob's life went smoothly after his mother conspired and robbed Esau of his birthright. Let's not lose track, however; that veiled in her action was God's divine plan at work. Throughout Jacob's life, he lived with the scars and stigma of a cheater and deceiver. I am sure he did not have answers to some of the questions he faced. I believe he often asked himself why.

Time and again, God showed up and did something miraculous that gave him hope to keep going. His life of complications continued into the life of Joseph. At the end of Jacob's life, the pieces were put together so we can learn from history that God is past finding out. God is not obligated to give us blueprints of the journey he has carved out for us. Even if God did, man's finite minds would not be able to comprehend the infinite things of God. If God showed us the path he designed for us, we would run away because we would be too scared to look ahead at what is in our path, though we might like the result when the journey is complete. It has been the pattern God used in history in taking his people along their journey step by step without telling them about their next experience. Jesus made a general statement about Saul, who we know as Paul. Here is what the Lord told Ananias about him, "…Go thy way: for he is a chosen vessel unto me, to bear my name before the Gentiles, and kings, and the children of Israel: For I will shew him how great things he must suffer for my name's sake" (Acts 9:15-16). That was a scary thought, but God had prepared him mentally, emotionally, spiritually, intellectually, psychologically, and physically. He did not know what the suffering would be as he journeyed, but looking back, he gave a synopsis to glimpse it, as recorded in 2 Corinthians 11:23-27. Despite those horrible experiences, he concluded that he had fought a good fight, kept the faith, and would be rewarded with a crown of righteousness. It is not until you can look back, retrace your steps, where God brought you from, and what the journey was like that you can appreciate God's wisdom and guiding hands.

It is like a child whose parent chastised him out of love, established boundaries that the child should not cross, and removed privileges if guidelines and protocols were not followed. That child resents and rebels against such corrections and restrictions until he can look back and appreciate what his parent has done to guide him along life's path by shielding him from danger. What you have been through, are going through, or will go through might be difficult to bear, but remember, your journey is not your destination; but you cannot get to your destination unless you take your journey. Your scars might not be in disguise, but you have been healed. You may have an ugly past, but your past is history. If one's past automatically determines the future, the redemptive blood of Christ would be of no effect. It also means that few people can move forward in life. Show me a man without scars, and I will show you someone who has never faced the real world. You cannot walk in the rain and never get wet. You can never fall on rocks and walk away without bruises. The apostle Paul, who wrote thirteen of the epistles (fourteen if we include Hebrews), would not have a chance. For many of us, who we were is not who we are and certainly not who we will be by God's grace.

The stories of many great men and women who have climbed the ladder of success defy the notion that one's history determines one's future. Sometimes, it becomes difficult to move forward because of our consciousness of guilt and the feeling that we have let down those who trusted us. However, do not hold yourself hostage to your past; your scars are reminders of your journey and experiences. They are not there to determine who you are currently. God saw your scars, knew where you are coming from, where you are, and what you will experience as you move forward, yet he has chosen to extend his grace to you and to make something beautiful out of you. God gave Jeremiah an example and insight into the work of the potter. He showed him how the clay gets marred right in the hand of the potter while on the potter's wheel. However, the potter does not throw the clay away. He remakes it and sometimes reshapes it into another vessel as it pleases him. You may be knocked out of shape and feel like you can never be what God intended. That could be an illusion, a figment of your imagination, or wishful thinking. What you are sure of today is who you are, where you are, and what God wants to do with and through you.

Hold your head up high and keep going forward. Where you are going far outweighs the importance of where you are coming from. Where you come from is history, but where you go from here is destiny; stay focused. There is a relevant reason a windshield is a hundred times (or more) the size of a rearview mirror. One of the reasons is not simply to protect you from the wind but to encourage you to keep your eyes on the big picture ahead and where you are going and to only glance at where you are coming from or what is behind you.

Develop the attitude of the man at the pool of Bethesda. He did not succumb to the pressure of the religious leaders and critics. He recognized that his future was more important than religious order or practices. His response to those who confronted him was following Christ's direction. "He answered them, He that made me whole, the same said unto me, take up thy bed and walk." The story is in John 5.

Do not allow others to hold you hostage to your past mentally, emotionally, socially, relationally, or spiritually. Do not hold yourself hostage, either. When God forgives you, forgive yourself and move forward. Scars are reminders of what you have been through, not to determine your future. Everyone born in this human flesh comes into the world with baggage. That recognition was part of David's prayer of confession and supplication to God. His cry was, "Behold, I was shapen in iniquity; and in sin did my mother conceive me" (Psalm 51:5). Flawlessness and perfection are not necessarily what God is looking for. Instead, he is looking for the broken to be a testimony of his power to mend broken hearts. God is looking for the battered and bruised to talk about the healing power of Christ.

Those whose lives have been deeply rooted in sin, who feel like they are too far away, he wants to make an example of the potency and efficacy of his redemptive blood. I pray that these examples mentioned in this book will inspire you to live above what others feel or think of you. Remember that the scars you wore or are wearing might be for God's glory. Say it like the apostle Paul, "...Most gladly therefore will I rather glory in my infirmities, that the power of Christ may rest upon me. Therefore I take pleasure in infirmities, in reproaches, in necessities, in persecutions, in distresses for Christ's sake: for when I am weak, then am I strong" (2 Corinthians 12:9-10).

It's hard to make sense of a situation while you're in it. Looking forward to what the end may be could be complicated and undiscernible. However, those who trust the Lord and have confidence in his wisdom and power will stretch their hands and ask him to lead them through the dark valleys of uncertainties, knowing that he can never fail and will not leave them to fend for themselves. I hope that this book has been a source of inspiration to you and helps you make sense of whatever you have been through, going through, or preparing you for the unknowns ahead. Not knowing what is ahead can make one apprehensive. But learning what others have been through may work as a template as you move forward. Having the understanding that one's experiences are not unique and exclusive helps build confidence.

ABOUT THE AUTHOR

Dr. Orville R. Beckford Sr. is an esteemed Bishop, theologian, and author, celebrated for his profound insights and transformative teachings. With a distinguished legacy spanning over four decades, Dr. Beckford has dedicated his life to the pastoral mission of nurturing spiritual growth and building deeply supportive and vibrant faith communities. His empathetic leadership, deep wisdom, and tireless work have earned him a reputation as a compassionate mentor and a visionary leader among his peers.

Born and raised in St. Andrew, Jamaica, Dr. Beckford discovered his calling at a young age. His journey of faith led him to pursue theological studies, culminating in a Ph.D. in Theology. His rigorous academic preparation combined with extensive practical experience has equipped him with a unique perspective on the intersection of historical context and contemporary spirituality. His book, The Seven Churches of Asia Minor, for example, is a masterful and engaging exploration of early Christian communities and their historical and spiritual significance to modern faith.

In his latest book, *Don't Judge Me by My Scars or Hold me Hostage to My Past*, Beckford delivers a poignant message that emphasizes the personal growth, healing, and hope that can be found in life's most challenging moments - moments which often leave visible and invisible scars. Drawing from theological wisdom and his own experiences, he crafts a compelling narrative that urges readers to suspend superficial judgments and appreciate the strength and growth that scars represent. By inviting readers to embrace the deep, transformative stories that emerge from the scars borne by others, Beckford's work becomes a call to compassion and understanding that uplifts entire communities.

Dr. Beckford's contributions extend beyond his writing; he is an impassioned speaker and mentor, touching countless lives with his profound insights and empathetic guidance. Through his teachings, writings, and community outreach, Dr. Beckford remains a beacon of hope and inspiration, guiding countless individuals toward a richer, more profound understanding of their faith and themselves. Through his unwavering commitment to faith and community, he continues to light the way for those navigating the often-challenging landscapes of life.

Together with his beloved wife Deana, Beckford continues to serve as Senior Pastor of Grace New Life Center COGOP in New Rochelle, New York.

Marlene Collins-Blair Ph.D

Made in the USA
Middletown, DE
16 October 2024